TRAVELLING TREASURES 2.0

Mala Kumar is a Bengaluru-based writer and editor. Author of *Travelling Treasures: 100 Incredible Tales of How Things Came to India*, *The Missing Rocks of Hampi*, *Up the Mountains of India*, *Crazy Mazy's Maths Puzzles* and many picture books, she loves engaging with children of all ages. An ardent sky and tree gazer, she spends her free time talking to children, cats, dogs, plants and writing occasional articles for newspapers about the good things she sees around her.

Also by the author:

TRAVELLING TREASURES 2.0

75 Incredible Tales of Things India Gave to the World

MALA KUMAR

Illustrated by Vibha Surya

hachette INDIA

First published in 2026 by Hachette India
(Registered name: Hachette Book Publishing India Pvt. Ltd)
An Hachette UK company
www.hachetteindia.com

1

ISBN: 978-93-5731-480-0

Hachette Book Publishing India Pvt. Ltd
4th & 5th Floors, Corporate Centre
Plot No. 94, Sector 44, Gurugram – 122003, India

Typeset by Manmohan Kumar, Delhi

Printed and bound in India
by Manipal Technologies Limited

MIX
Paper | Supporting responsible forestry
FSC™ C043100
FSC www.fsc.org

For Aarav and Ved, Elena and Caterina,
and for children everywhere.
Live with curiosity, let live with respect, share with grace.

CONTENTS

INTRODUCTION

When you gaze at the map of the world, and stroke your chin a bit, many questions may arise in your mind. One that comes to my mind quite often is, how is it that for many of us in the city, walking from home to the metro station seems like an ordeal, while people living hundreds of years ago made no fuss about walking alongside their camels for days or riding upon horseback for weeks or sailing for months just to get things like buttons and pepper? Another question that arises is, how did countries learn about each other? How did India become such an important part of global trade routes?

Humans have always been wanting the next best thing. Have fire-starting stones? Want matchsticks. Have cycle? Want motorbike. Have pencil? Want pen. Have mango? Want peach. Have gold? Want rubies. And that is how trade began. Over time, as each region of the world discovered its own resources, so did the lure for goods that were not available. Imagine if you were a farmer and grew only cabbages – would you survive on just cabbage? The least you would need to make it a palatable dish is a pinch of salt, a shake of pepper and a twist of lemon. What if your region had no lemons?

And so, brave traders went from one country to another, trading gold for pepper, maybe apples for oranges, paper for silver and so on. *Travelling Treasures: 100 Incredible Tales of How Things Came to India* tells the stories of how ordinary things made extraordinary journeys from across the world to reach India. In *Travelling Treasures* 2.0, it's India's turn to travel as we discover how things went out into the world, either directly from or through India before the creation of the democratic republic of India on 15 August 1947.

The entries in this book are based on their origin; or the origin of their importance; or their domestication; or their trade in India. But what is India? If India's borders were drawn only in 1947 (a bit of unfinished business there), and if the name 'India' and 'Bharat' were enshrined in our Constitution only in 1949, what was the boundary of India before that? The subcontinent was actually a group of kingdoms with no single ruler or ruling government. There were no official boundaries for India as a whole. Different people referred to this land differently. In the Rig Veda (more about that when you get to V for Vedas), the river after which India gets its name is called Sindhu. Most people understood India or Bharatavarsha loosely as the region 'south of the Sindhu River, stretching up to Cape Comorin (now Kanniyakumari) and between the Arabian Sea and the Bay of Bengal'. Our neighbours in the west pronounced Sindhu as Hindu in Persian and Arabic. The Greeks made it Indus, dropping the 'H'. In Old English, influenced by the French, it became Ynde or Inde. And from that, the people of Inde began to be called Indian. And the land came to be called India in the Western world.

History is an ever-evolving field. What is taken as fact today may not be true when an archaeologist digs up a new bone – or rather, a very ancient bone that changes the existing fact. Historians do tons of work before arriving at any conclusion. And yet, different historians come to different conclusions. Did Kautilya, alias Chanakya, exist? Did he really create the *Arthashastra*? You see, there is no direct evidence of his existence, and yet we believe he existed because of narratives coming from four different sources.

India gave the world diamonds (actually, the art of mining diamonds), ivory, pepper and badminton. While these are precious, what are even more valuable are the philosophies, ideas, art and literature that originated in the Indian subcontinent. For example, practices like yoga and concepts such as ahimsa have travelled far beyond their origins, becoming part of everyday global vocabulary and lifestyle.

India is an extraordinary country – you already know that! Much of our ancient knowledge about the sciences, literature and philosophy has been lost forever. But what remains is still a stupendous gift from the past to us. Now, that gift is in your hands, to use and to share with the world. Just like how the treasures from around the world make our life richer, the treasures from India have and can continue to make the world a better place.

Now it's time to start the journey. You can read from the beginning or from anywhere in the book. But if you do plan to start with A, do keep a pinch of salt handy!

Tigers and Tell-Tale Signs

History is a huge and labouriously made patchwork of data collected from different sources. Books written by travellers make up most of these patches. Strabo, the Greek geographer and author of the 17-book set called *Geographica*, wrote about the Roman king Augustus (who reigned between 27 BCE–14 CE) and how he improved trade with the East (that includes India). The number of ships sailing to India increased from 20 to over 120 vessels during that time. From India, spices, fabrics, precious stones and exotic animals, like tigers, were taken to be sold to the rich in the Mediterranean world. Golden coins minted in Brundisium (Brindisi, in southern Italy), dated 27 BCE, were found in Pudukkottai, Tamil Nadu. (How did the coins reach there? Another story for another time, maybe.) Historians have found evidence of India's traders doing business as early as the 7th millennium BCE (that's at least 8,000 years ago). Indian merchants were travelling from India with goods that could be traded for gems called lapis in Afghanistan which were then taken to Syria. We know all this from the tell-tale signs left by the people of those times in the form of inscriptions, coins, objects, art and architecture.

AMLA

According to Hindu mythology, the amla berry grew on the first tree that came up when Brahma, the creator god, was meditating. His tears of devotion rolled down to the ground, giving birth to the amla tree. Science tells us that most gooseberries belong to one of three basic varieties, the European *Ribes uva-crispa*, the North American *Ribes hirtellum* or the Indian *Phyllanthus emblica* (also, *Emblica officinalis*). Most people would agree that amla, as the Indian gooseberry is called, is a 'super berry'.

How super? One amla has more vitamin C than three oranges or sixteen bananas! (We're not talking here about *Phyllanthus acidus*, the smaller and sweeter gooseberry, that grows in clusters which could have come to India from Madagascar.) *Phyllanthus emblica* is a small tree that grows all over India. It is native to India and many other parts of South Asia. It can grow even in wastelands. The sour berry is an excellent antioxidant. Antioxidants are molecules that fight free radicals – you could think of them as the naughty molecules that float around and cause diseases. Amla is one of the primary ingredients in the Ayurvedic preparation called *chyawanprash*, made with at least 50 ingredients.

That the berry was considered precious is highlighted even in literature. According to a verse in the Sanskrit text *Ashokavadana*, when the Mauryan emperor Ashoka renounced his kingdom in around 260 BCE, his final gift to the Buddhist sangha was half an *amalaka*, or amla. When Avvaiyar, a renowned Tamil poetess, was a guest of Adhiyaman Neduman Anji, the king of the South Indian kingdom, he presented her with many things, including a rare kind of gooseberry. He was such a great patron of the Tamil language that he believed the amla would keep the poetess, and therefore the language, healthy for a long time.

The Persian writer Al-Biruni, knowledgeable in many subjects including mathematics, science and astronomy, learnt about the health benefits of amla during his thirteen-year stay in India. He wrote about it in his book on medicine, *Kitab al-Saydanah fi al-Tibb*. Amla's fame thus spread to Persia and beyond.

India is the largest producer of amla. The berry in its many forms and its extracts are exported to many countries. Amla is not only used in traditional medicines, but also made into morabba, pickles, jams and mouth fresheners. While the Indian gooseberry is not too familiar outside the country, there are people all over the world who enjoy these treats.

By the way, the town called Amla in Madhya Pradesh was named after... no, not the amla, but the *aam* or mango. (Please do not get into an argument with people who think the place got its name as a backronym created by the British for AMunition LAnd!)

ARABIC NUMERALS

Are numbers and numerals the same? A number is an abstract idea of quantity. The answer to 'How many chocolates did you eat today?' is a number. Numeral is the symbol you use to represent that answer, say 3. So, 3 is a numeral. You could also answer with three claps of your hands, or hold up three fingers. Which, of course, are not numerals.

Numbers and counting have been part of human evolution for at least 40,000 years. People kept score in many ways, including making marks on cave walls and sticks. One of the oldest mathematical artefacts in the world is the Lebombo bone, a piece of a baboon's fibula with 29 distinctive markings. It is believed to have been used as a tally stick and could be anywhere from 36,000 to 42,000 years old! People used their fingers and other body parts to count numbers. They did not have symbols to represent each of the numbers they knew. So, while the history of numbers is pre-historic really, the history of numerals is quite recent by comparison.

Researchers have found over a hundred different systems of writing numbers in the past 5,000 years. The earliest clear notations to represent numbers, maybe 5,000–6,000 years ago, are from Mesopotamia. Roman numerals were invented somewhere in the first millennium BCE. But this system had no sign for zero. Also, it was pretty difficult to do mathematical operations, though the ancient world did an astonishing number of calculations.

It was only between the 1st and 4th centuries CE that Indian mathematicians worked on a system of numbers that is the direct ancestor of the system of numerals we use across the world today. These were written down in Brahmi script in the 3rd century in present-day Bihar. In parallel, Aryabhata, in his book *Aryabhatiya* described a system where each consonant of the Sanskrit alphabet represented a different number. By 600 CE, Indians were using numerals to represent 1 to 9. By 625 CE, the concept of 'nothing' or *shunya* came to be. It was used as a placeholder in the base-10 system. Indian astronomer Brahmagupta was the first to meditate on the nature of *shunya*, probably sitting on a hill in Mount Abu, his native place. He came up with its properties, giving it the status of the tenth numeral. (More about zero, the mathematical hero, on page 199.)

The Arabs soaked in Indian theories, improved and corrected ancient Greek texts, and added their own to discover many mathematical truths. The Arabs improved the Brahmi Indian numerals, and the modern numerals were born. They called it Hindu numerals. Even before this, Syrian priest Severus Sebokht wrote with great admiration about 'the nine signs' of the Indians. A brilliant mathematician called Muhammad ibn Musa al-Khwarizmi wrote *The Book on Addition and Subtraction After the Method of the Indians*, which was translated into Latin in the 12th century. This was an important introduction of the numerals to Europe. It wasn't taken too seriously, though. Earlier too, in Albelda,

Spain, a monk called Vigila had written about the talent of Indians for devising the nine figures.

Meanwhile, Leonardo of Pisa, the Italian mathematician born in 1170, learnt Arabic, learnt the systems of numerals and, in 1202, wrote the book *Liber Abaci*. Known by the name Fibonacci (you'll know why if you turn to page 75), he popularized the Arabian numerals in Europe. Leonardo wrote about his introduction to a wonderful kind of teaching that used the nine figures of the Indians. He mentioned that with the sign 0, which the Arabs call 'al-sifr' any number could be written.

While the Romans were reluctant to accept a system from the Arabian world, they eventually saw the beauty and practicality of using these numerals. After the invention of the printing press in around 1440, mathematical symbols and numerals were standardized. Hindu-Arabic or Indo-Arabic numerals, born in India and improved by the Arabians, had become the common language of the world.

ASTRONOMY

Astrology and astronomy are often used interchangeably. Both are the study of celestial objects. It was only in the medieval times that they were recognized as two different fields of study. Astronomy was based on mathematical theories and precise measurements, while astrology was the study of first observing and then interpreting the magical elements to make predictions for humans. Astrology worked on the principle that what was above would affect what is below. The two fields are linked because both rely on observing celestial patterns. Humans must have started observing astronomical cycles very early in their evolution. Who wouldn't have noticed the movement of the sun every day, or the moon's phases over a month.

Astronomy was well-known in the Vedic times in India. Astronomical information helped farmers in planning the cycles of sowing and reaping. It was also used to prepare for Vedic rituals. Throughout history and almost till the 17th century, astrology was studied across Eurasia.

The earliest documented literature about astronomy, however, is available only from around circa 1180 BCE when the teachings of sage Lagadha were compiled as the *Vedanga Jyotisa*. Greek astronomical knowledge started entering

India in the 4th century BCE, during the time of Alexander. Varāhamihira, an astronomer of Ujjain in present-day Madhya Pradesh, discovered many astronomical calculations around 505 CE. He studied principles of Roman, Egyptian and Greek astronomical sciences, learning from all directions. Aryabhata (476 CE–550 CE), in his book *Aryabhatiya*, wrote about the cause of day and night, and the methods of determining the positions of planets. While he did not propose the heliocentric model of the solar system, he did provide the mathematical proof that the Earth was a spinning sphere in space. This is the first step towards the heliocentric theory, proposed more than 1,000 years before the Polish polymath Nicolaus Copernicus did! The great astronomer Aryabhata was followed by Bhaskara in the 7th century CE, and Lalla in the 8th century CE.

From 250 BCE to 1200 CE, India's ideas, arts and knowledge kept spreading on both sides of the subcontinent. Ideas about celestial objects moved eastwards to the court of Empress Wu Zetian (624 CE–705 CE), the first and only woman ruler of a Chinese kingdom, from Nalanda, Kanchipuram and Ceylon (now Sri Lanka). Muslim scientists recognized the importance of Brahmagupta's Sanskrit text about astronomy, *Brahmasphutasiddhanta*, which he wrote when he was just 30 years old. Later, in his sixties, he wrote another manual on Indian astronomy. At some point, the two books may have become one. The scholars in the Middle East heard about this work. Arab philosopher, mathematician and astronomer Muhammad al-Fazārī (746 CE–806 CE) translated the book into Arabic, which became popular as *The Great Sindhind*. This translation led to many other discoveries in mathematics and astronomy. In Toledo, in 11th-century Spain, it was also translated into

Latin and Hebrew. In the 10th–11th centuries, another famous Arab, Al-Biruni made the distinction between astrology and astronomy, and carried forward the science of Indo-Islamic origin.

The importance of learning different languages becomes clear when one reads about people like Michael Scot (1175 CE–1232 CE) who translated Indo-Islamic work from Arabic to Latin and helped take the learnings to Christian Europe. If you have a flair for languages, you should definitely aim to be a polyglot.

Today, India continues to observe, study and discover the magic of astronomy. In 2025, Indian scientists at the National Centre for Radio Astrophysics of the Tata Institute of Fundamental Research (NCRA-TIFR) in Pune discovered a massive galaxy that was formed when the universe as we know it was just – just? – 1.5 billion years old. They named it Alaknanda, after the Himalayan river.

Astronomy Quiz

1. What's a quake on the moon called?
2. What possible astronomical structure was found in Dholavira, a Harappan site in Gujarat?
3. Which Indian scholar was the first to propose that Earth rotated on its axis?

Answers: 1. Moonquake 2. A celestial observatory 3. Aryabhata

AYURVEDA

When you have a cough, you've probably been told to pluck a few leaves of tulsi and chew on it. Or maybe, someone in your family boiled a few leaves of tulsi in water, added some honey to it and gave you the decoction to drink. What a relief! Where do you think the recipe for this genius cough syrup came from? From Ayurveda, of course.

Ayurveda literally means 'the knowledge of life' in Old Sanskrit. 'Ayur' means life and 'veda' means knowledge. Ayurveda is a system of healthcare that is based on the belief that *prakriti* (the natural constituents of the body) and *dosha* (the various forces of life) are interconnected. In Ayurveda, it is believed that humans are made up of five elements – earth, water, fire, air and ether. Each of us has a different proportion of these elements, giving us one of three broad types of constitutions called *vata*, *pitta* and *kapha*. An imbalance in one part of the body affects another. This causes illness. By understanding our bodies and learning what type of *dosha* we have, Ayurveda prescribes a way of life that not only prevents disease but also helps to fight illness. More than medicines it is nutrition, lifestyle and natural treatment that keeps us healthy.

Ayurveda is an ancient system, and no one knows who came up with it first. According to mythology, it was Brahma, the god of creation, who first came up with the system. Did Brahma reveal it to Dhanvantari, the god of health? Or did Brahma reveal it to his son Daksha Prajapati who passed it on to sun god Surya's sons, the Asvini brothers? While there are varying answers to such questions, the first mention of Ayurveda is in the *Atharvaveda*, which was created somewhere in the 2nd millennium BCE. That is, roughly 3,000 years ago!

First, Sage Agnivesha is believed to have created an encyclopaedia on Ayurveda called *Agnivesha Samhita.* Years later, Sage Charaka edited it, and it came to be called *Charaka Samhita.* In the 4th century CE, Dridhabala, an ayurvedic scholar in the Kashmir region reconstructed many lost chapters. This was the text that physicians in India referred to. The other important document is the *Sushruta Samhita*, in which the physician Sushruta describes 121 different surgical instruments. He practised in the ancient city of Kashi (now Varanasi) around 600 BCE, and earned the title 'Father of Surgery'. The oldest surviving palm-leaf manuscript of this work, written in the Kutila script, is preserved at the Kaiser Library in Kathmandu, Nepal.

Though most cultures in Asia had their own systems of medicine, Ayurveda influenced many of them including those of Tibet, Central Asia, China, Southeast Asia and the Middle East. The Arabic translation of the *Sushruta Samhita* was commissioned by the Kaliph Al-Mansur in the 7th century. Called *Kelale-Shawshoore-al-Hindi*, this translation was later translated into Latin. The gathering of international scholars at the ancient Nalanda University helped to spread the knowledge about the Ayurvedic system of healthcare to many places.

In the 16th and 17th centuries, Portuguese and Dutch physicians introduced many elements of Ayurveda's standards to European medical knowledge. The cross-pollination of knowledge also enriched Ayurveda. In 1822, the British rulers in India set up the Native Medical Institution in Calcutta (now Kolkata) to train young Indians in both Western and indigenous medical systems. A few years later, the Institution also encouraged the teaching of Ayurveda in Sanskrit colleges and of Unani medicine in madrasas. But by 1835, with a new head who favoured Western medicine, the Native Medical Institution was closed, and the Ayurveda and Unani medical education was stopped. The Ayurvedic medicines were categorized using European standards, and instead of herbs, the prescriptions mentioned the chemicals associated with them. All these factors led to the decline of Ayurveda and the growth of Western medicine.

After India's Independence, Ayurveda began to flourish again. Today, Ayurveda has followers all over the world. In the United States of America, for instance, Ayurveda has been found to be one of the most popular alternative medical systems recognized by the US National Center for Complementary and Integrative Health (NCCIH), formerly the NCCAM. People who follow Ayurveda do it to maintain a balance between the body, mind and spirit. Ayurveda is not just about medicines but a 'way of living'. Stay active, rest enough, eat a balanced meal, show gratitude for the food you eat and listen to your body. That is what Ayurveda suggests. So, it is good news that as per the 2026–27 Union budget, India plans to open more Ayurvedic institutes to strengthen education, clinical services and research. It also aims to have more international collaborations to promote traditional medicine, including Sowa Rigpa. What's that? An Indo-Tibetan medical system that grew out of Ayurveda!

BADMINTON

In 2023, Satwiksairaj Rankireddy recorded the fastest smash on a badminton court with his shuttle recording a speed of 565 km/hour. In comparison, the highest speed of a Formula 1 car at that time was less than 400 km/hr!

But wait, first let's do a fast rewind and find out how the game of badminton was born. A version of the game is believed to have been played in ancient India, Greece and China over 2,000 years ago. The Chinese called their game, ti zian ji, and it involved keeping the shuttlecock in the air by kicking it. No racket? Then we can't call it badminton, can we? In medieval Europe (that's roughly 5th century CE to 15th century CE), children played a game called battledore and shuttlecock, and in the 17th century, there was a similar game called jeu de volant. All these involved feathers stuck to a piece of cork.

It was in the 19th century during the British rule in India that shuttlecock really took on its modern ways. The British officers working here started playing the game during their leisure hours. The soldiers stationed in Poona (now Pune) added some rules that included having a net. They started calling the game Poonah. In southern India, the same game used to be played with a woollen ball instead of a shuttle.

So, the game now had two variants, one for normal weather with the shuttlecock, and the other for wet and windy weather with the woollen ball. When the officers returned to England, they continued to play the game with its new rules. In 1873, the Duke of Beaufort threw a party in his estate in Gloucestershire, in the village of Badminton. His estate was called Badminton House. When he introduced the game formally to his guests, he called it badminton. The name stuck, and the game was set.

The game caught on, and the Bath Badminton Club was set up in 1877. The Badminton Association of India was formed in 1934. Badminton was introduced as an Olympic game in 1992. Indian shuttlers have done us proud, starting with Prakash Padukone who was the first Indian to make it to the top 10 in the world. P.V. Sindhu was India's first world champion, and her two Olympic medals are lovely feathers in her cap.

Speaking of feathers, the shuttlecock has a curious legend behind its existence. According to this popular myth, in the olden days when people used feathers to write with, they needed a place to park them, and a piece of cork would serve the purpose. Soon, like naughty people do, the cork pen-stand with its stuck feathers, was being flung around, and they made a game of whacking it from here to there using paddles and boards. There is no proof of this origin, though.

Now, while a lot of plastic shuttlecocks are in use, professionals still use shuttlecocks made with high-quality cork and duck or goose feathers of the same size and shape. In fact, all sixteen feathers are taken from the same side of the wing, because feathers of the right wing can make the shuttlecock swing in a different way from the feathers of the left wing. And if both right wing and left wing feathers are used in the same shuttle, the flight and spin of the shuttlecock would not be ideal.

There's nothing like a game of badminton to keep one fit since it involves running, diving, stretching, hitting, jumping and bending. Point taken?

BHAGAVAD GITA

Imagine the scene. A battlefield with an army of soldiers, horses and elephants on both sides. This is Kurukshetra. Arjuna, one of the five Pandavas, is in his chariot drawn by none other than the great Krishna, his cousin. Arjuna has a moral dilemma – should he follow his duty as a soldier, or should he refuse to fight his own blood, family and teachers? Which path should he take? Krishna tells him to do his duty, to fight the war and bring peace. You would think it would be a short, sharp, smart order, right? Instead, Krishna's advice is more of a long conversation with Arjuna. When written down, this advice ran to 18 *parvas*, or chapters, with 700 slokas! This is the Bhagavad Gita, 'the Song of the Lord'.

The Bhagavad Gita, or the Gita for short, has been part of India for over 2,500 years. It is a tiny part of a poem called 'Jaya' composed by the sage Vyasa. Many years later, it was recited by Vyasa rishi's disciple, Sage Vaishampayana, to the great-grandson of Arjuna, King Janamejaya. This version was called 'Bharata'. Over the years, the composition kept growing. When the travelling storyteller Ugrashrava Sauti narrated it to a few sages, it had 1,00,000 slokas and came to be called the Mahabharata.

The first written version of the Mahabharata with the Gita within it is probably just 1,700 years old, created somewhere in the 4th century CE. The message in the Bhagavad Gita was so simple and powerful that it continued to inspire people to do their duty. Everyone who learnt about the Gita realized that the message in it was universal.

By the 7th century CE, Java and Sumatra, two islands of Indonesia, had Hindu–Buddhist rulers. The Mahabharata – including the Gita, of course – became a part of the culture of the region, being seen as an important text rather than just a religious text. As Hinduism and Buddhism spread to South Asia, so did references from the Mahabharata. The epic inspired the creation of many literary and theatrical works in Burma (now Myanmar), Thailand, Malaysia, Cambodia and Indonesia.

Al-Biruni, the great Khwarazmian Iranian polymath and scientist, was the first to introduce the study of Bhagavad Gita to the Muslim world. (He also studied the Puranas and was the first Muslim to translate many Sanskrit texts dealing with astronomy, mathematics, geography and medicine.)

Hikayat Perang Pandawa Jaya is the Malay version of the Mahabharata written between 14th–16th century CE. It was adapted from the Javanese derivation called *Bharatayuddha*.

The first English translation of the Bhagavad Gita was by Charles Wilkins, a British co-founder of the Asiatic Society in Calcutta in 1785. It influenced poets like William Blake, Wordsworth, Yeats and Coleridge. American poets Thoreau, Emerson and others too were inspired by it. It was translated into many other languages, making it known to the whole world.

Irrespective of religion, nationality or race, people have tried to follow the teachings expressed in the Gita.

If read carefully, and understood properly, this manual from ancient India can shape how we think, feel, live and express ourselves.

On 17 April 2025, the Bhagavad Gita was added to UNESCO's Memory of the World Register. This is an initiative that collects and preserves the documentary heritage of global importance.

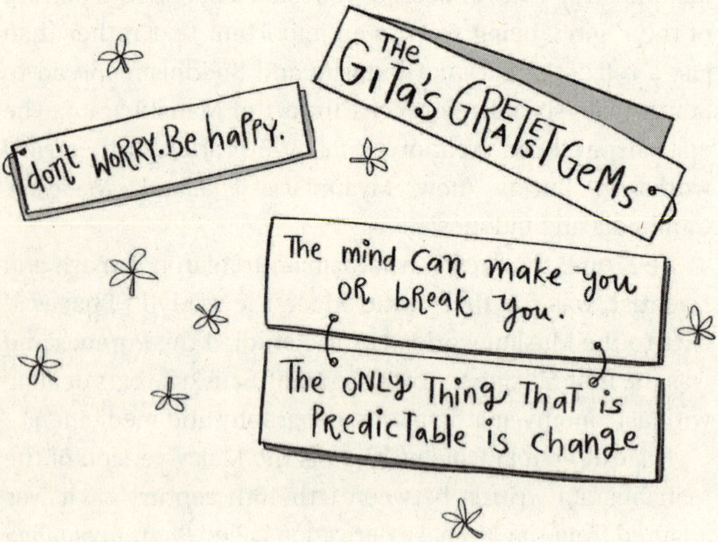

BHARATANATYAM

Among the many Sanskrit texts that are still studied by students of the performing arts is the *Natyashastra*. It is the oldest surviving encyclopaedia of India's performing arts dated between the 2nd century BCE and the 4th century BCE. In this Sanskrit text you will find no mention of Bharatanatyam! Why? Because the dance form was not called by that name then. No one knows when it began, but all research leads to the conclusion that it started in South India, and was called by the names *dasi attam* or *sadir* and later, *karnatakam*. But it was given a formal structure by the Thanjavur Quartet – brothers Chinnayya, Ponnayya, Sivanandam and Vadivelu, born between 1802 and 1810. Musicians and dancers of the Brihadeeswara Temple lineage, they performed at the court of the Maratha ruler Serfoji II in Thanjavur. They composed many songs in Telugu, especially suited for dance. So well-known was their talent and dedication that the kings of Travancore and Mysore also invited them to perform and heaped gifts on them.

The members of the East India Company did not understand the spiritual roots of this dance form and had it banned in 1910. But brave Indians, proud of their heritage, continued to dance. Thanjavur Balasaraswathi was one of them. In 1934, she danced in the Bharatanatyam style to 'Jana gana mana', in the presence of its creator Rabindranath Tagore. Of course, it had not yet been adopted as the Indian National Anthem then. Dancers like Rukmini Devi Arundale fought to revive Bharatanatyam, and in 1936, with the help of her husband – British-born George Arundale – she founded Kalakshetra in Madras (now Chennai).

As interest in the 'exotic East' spread in the faraway Western world, Indian dance forms became known abroad. Dancers like Esther Luella Sherman learnt and performed in New York as early as 1922, borrowing moves from Bharatanatyam and other dance forms. She took the stage name Ragini Devi, moved to India and learnt Bharatanatyam, Mohiniattam and Kalaripayattu from different gurus.

In 1932, members of the Music Academy of Madras suggested calling the ancient temple dance of *sadir* as Bharatanatyam. It was a move to give the dance form the respectability and credit it deserved. While there was never a formal naming ceremony or event, the name stuck, and art lovers continue to appreciate this dance of discipline, expression, artistic heritage and beauty.

BINDI

The bindi comes from the Sanskrit word 'bindu', meaning a dot. There are many theories about why people wear a bindi – or pottu, bottu, phot, phut, tilak, teeka, tilakam, tilaka, as it is known in different languages. It was a custom even in the Indus Valley Civilization (IVC), over 4,000 years ago. Terracotta figurines believed to be from 2800 BCE found in Naushahro Feroze, now in Pakistan, show what could be a mark of kumkum on the hair parting above the forehead. Archaeologists in Afghanistan found a gold figurine dating back to the 1st century BCE, of Aphrodite of Bactria, with a bindi on the forehead. Of course, people of those times could not rip a bindi off a plastic sheet and stick it between their brows. They would have had to use leaves or flowers, or make a paste of turmeric or sandalwood. Why did they do it?

Let's think. To think well, you have to close your eyes, and touch your forehead, or drum on it with your fingers, or rub it. Right? At the centre of the forehead is a spot where the mind and senses are believed to meet, called the third eye. It was believed that activating that point helped humans to look within themselves, to concentrate and to calmly find solutions. It is also called the ajna chakra, one of the six chakras or energy centres in the human body as per ancient Hindu and Buddhist traditions. Could the practice of applying a bindi be an attempt to activate this chakra? Many practitioners believe so.

And then there is the tiny, rice-sized, pinecone-shaped pineal gland in the centre of our brain, some 12 cm behind the centre of our forehead. This gland regulates our sleep cycle. While there is no scientific proof yet, the ancient Indians, Greeks, Taoists and Egyptians believed that activating this gland had many benefits. Many people believe that the mindful act of applying a bindi (notice, we aren't saying sticking a bindi!) stimulates this gland. Though largely seen as a Hindu tradition, people of different faiths including Parsis, Muslims, Sikhs and Christians have a tradition of wearing bindis.

Bindis are also worn by women in countries like Indonesia which had Hindu kings in the past. Early travellers from China like Buddhist monks and scholars are believed to have carried the idea back to China too. China does have an ancient practice called the First Writing Ceremony or Qi Meng (meaning enlightenment). A red dot would be put on children's foreheads just before they began school . The vermilion dot represented the opening of the wisdom eye. The children would then honour philosopher and teacher Confucius, also called as Kongzi.

Kumkum was the powder used on the forehead by both men and women. The traditional recipe requires dry turmeric root to be soaked in a mixture of calcined borax, alum and lemon juice. The sun-dried turmeric is pounded and mixed with a little bit of sesame oil or ghee. The resultant powder is aromatic and anti-microbial, and believed to have a healing effect on the skin. This kumkum is also used in religious practices. Each region in India has its special addition to the mix, like the fragrant thazhampoo or screw-pine flower in Madurai and saffron in Kashmir.

Moving away from natural materials, bindis soon came to be made with plastic and shiny baubles. Bindis are now worn for religious and cultural reasons, and also as an adornment to beautify oneself. The idea of the bindi travelled and many celebrities in the West started sporting bindis, not just on their forehead but also around their eyebrows. This was their way of appreciating the Indian practice of wearing bindis. Have you seen pictures of rockstars and international models wearing them at music fests and global runaways?

THE HEROES OF THE INDUS VALLEY CIVILIZATION

The Indus Valley Civilization (IVC), now also called the Sindhu-Saraswati Civilization (SSC), is going to crop up many times in this book. The people of this civilization were awesome. The world did not know much about IVC because India started archaeological exercises only in the early 20th century, much later than other countries. This is why we hear a lot more about Egypt, Babylonia, Sumer and Mesopotamia than about our own civilization.

Humans have been living as a civilized settlement – meaning they have taken care of each other – in the Indian subcontinent for at least 9,000 years. We can say this because of the discoveries made at Mehrgarh (in Pakistan) and Bhirrana (in Haryana, India). In the late 1820s, a British soldier ran away from the army, changed his name to Charles Masson to avoid being caught and headed towards the Indus River in the west. There he stumbled upon a ruined citadel. He became the first person to find the ancient 'Haripah'. (Incidentally, Masson was a numismatist who had collected 47,000 coins. He also helped excavate many Buddhist sites.)

In 1842, Masson included his detailed notes about his findings at the site in his book *Narrative of Various Journeys in Balochistan, Afghanistan, and the Punjab.* Not knowing the importance of the site, people from nearby started taking away the bricks (more about them on page 29) that they found. The British overseers too allowed the use of these bricks to lay nearly 160 km of railway tracks between Multan and Lahore.

When Alexander Cunningham was appointed the Archaeological Surveyor in 1861, he set out hoping to prove that the site described by Masson was the lost Buddhist city described by Xuanzang in the 7th century. In his report, he wrote a short note on 'Harapa' but did not know about its importance.

Many decades later, excavations at Harappa were done by Rai Bahadur Daya Ram Sahni of the Archaeological Survey of India (ASI) in 1920. His colleague Madho Sarup Vats continued his work. Since the first site to be excavated was Harappa (just a kilometre away from the modern town of the same name in Pakistan), the civilization got the name Harappan. When Mohenjo-daro (also in present-day Pakistan) was discovered, also on the banks of the Indus, the civilization was called Indus Valley Civilization. Now, with more research, it has been found that the sites were not just near the Indus but also near the now-disappeared river Sarasvati. Hence the name Sindhu–Sarasvati Civilization.

The civilization is known for excellent city planning, sophisticated drainage systems, industrious trade and the invention of many toys – which showed that the people of IVC really cared about work-life balance enough to play with their children. That they traded with Mesopotamia is clear from the fact that Harappan jewellery was found in archaeological sites in modern-day Kuwait, Syria and Iraq. They knew how to travel on water and over land. Unfortunately, the civilization died down. No one knows exactly why, but climate change may have been one factor.

The Harappans are also believed to have a script – they did have at least 600 different symbols! No one has deciphered the IVC text yet. Maybe, you will one day soon. Once that is done, the world will know a lot more about our ancestors and what happened to them. You'll find more information about this ancient civilization scattered throughout this book.

The different periods of IVC are categorized like this:

Pre-Harappan – c. 7000–c. 5500 BCE

Early Harappan – c. 5500–c. 2800 BCE

Mature Harappan – c. 2600–c. 1900 BCE

Late Harappan – c. 1900–c. 1500 BCE

Post Harappan – c. 1500–c. 600 BCE

BIRYANI

Biryani is one of the most popular orders on Indian food apps. And guess which particular dish is most ordered secretly – that is, in incognito mode? Chicken biryani! Lovers of biryani do not care about its historical origin, or which country invented it. They just want to relish it. They may argue about who makes better biryani, or which flavour is better or whether the hot and spicy biryani is better than the lightly flavoured one. However, this book is about origins, and so we shall try to go to the origin of biryani.

Everyone agrees that biryani is a dish made with rice and spices, and with meat or vegetables, and that there are at least twenty-six distinct types popular in our country. There is also no doubt about the fact that it is an Asian preparation. West Asian or Indian? Now that is a tricky question. While no historian has yet reached the bottom of the pot on this controversy, there is a clear divide between people who think it was brought to India from the Middle East, and some others who staunchly believe it is a true-blue Indian invention. There is consensus that the word is of Persian origin. Biryani gets its name from the Persian *birinj*, meaning rice. It could also be from another Persian word *biryan* which means fried or roasted, especially fried onions. Oh, actually, wait! Some people say the Sanskrit word for rice, *vrihi* led to the word *birinj*. The debate is still raging on that issue.

Meanwhile, let's take you to an epic war story, the Mahabharata. You may know the part about the legendary king who disguised himself as a cook. King Nala was not only a great cook, but was also an efficient documenter, it seems. The Mahabharata mentions him as the cook who conjured the tastiest food for King Rituparna. He is credited with creating a treatise called *Pakadrapana*. It has eleven chapters and includes topics like how to choose ingredients, and how to be a good cook, apart from recipes of many dishes. One of them is the *mamsodana*, a dish made with rice and meat. Could this be one of the early variations of what later became famous as biryani? A similar dish called *harisha* is mentioned in *Bhojanakutuhala*, another treatise.

Let us not fight over the origin. Let us take a bay leaf from the life of the Chera king who earned the title 'Pernuchottru Uthiyan' (big feast Uthiyan). Why? Because he is believed to have fed the soldiers on both sides of a huge war, while staying neutral. The one-pot dish that was served was called *oon soru* and made with - you guessed it - rice, meat and spices. This dish was well-known during the Sangam period in the South.

As trade between countries increased, the food too was influenced by the flavours of different regions. The Mughal rulers in India added their own touch to the rice dish and traders took the idea on their travels. With time, each region of the country gave it its own twist. The biryani, as it came to be known, became popular across the world.

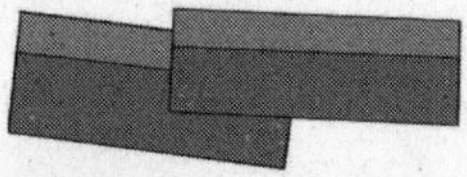

BRICKS

Bricks are such simple things that we don't really think of them much. But where would we be without them? Definitely not in a safe and strong brick-and-mortar bookshop, school, library or house! The earliest known bricks are from 7500 BCE. They were found in Çayönü in Southeast Anatolia, Türkiye. They were made with clay, fashioned by hand and left to dry in the sun. It was around 4500–3000 BCE that baked or fired bricks began to be used in the Indus Valley Civilization and in Mesopotamia. Fired bricks were stronger, and more resistant to water and sun and cold.

Ancient bricks found throughout the IVC region have the same measurements. Made with mud, they were all in the same ratio of 4:2:1 (length:width:height). While most of the bricks were sun-dried, the later ones were kiln-fired bricks. The bricks could be laid with an interlocking system – no need for cement! This led to the construction of more permanent structures like temples and palaces.

It was the discovery of these bricks during the excavation work for the Lahore-Multan railway line that led to the discovery of what came to be called the Indus Valley Civilization. Certainly, all the archaeologists who dug patiently for years and years deserve many bouquets, not brickbats.

BUDDHISM

The caves in Ajanta, in the forests of the Western Ghats, were discovered by a hunting party. It was later found out that these were some of the oldest human-made caves in the world. The next big surprise was the quality and nature of the beautiful murals inside the caves that depicted the life of Buddha. Painted in brilliant colours, they show court scenes, hunting scenes, blue lotuses, orange-robed monks and the two most beautiful Bodhisattvas, beings who are on the way to becoming enlightened. The most revered painting is the one showing the meditating Buddha.

Siddhartha Gautama was born a Shakya prince in Lumbini close to the then capital city Kapilavastu, in Nepal. While most historians agree that he was born in the 5th century BCE, his actual year of birth continues to be debated. As a young prince, he was educated in the arts and sciences (and which game is he believed to have played? Check page 93!). For 29 years he lived in the palace, but increasingly disturbed by the many questions he had, he set out on a path of discovery. He gave up his princely life, travelled, learnt from others and came to the conclusion that the only way for him was to follow the right spiritual path. But what was this path? First, he tried being an ascetic. He was not happy with this austere, very strict path. He started meditating. At the age of 35, while sitting under a *bodhi* tree (*Ficus religiosa*, also called peepal) in Gaya, Bihar, he is believed to have become the enlightened one, the Buddha.

The Buddha gave his first public sermon in Sarnath, Uttar Pradesh. He talked about the four truths for the noble, which in the Pali language are *dukkha* (the feeling of unsatisfactoriness), *samudaya* (origin of suffering), *nirodha* (stopping of the suffering) and *magga* (the path to stop the suffering). This became the basis of a religion called Buddhism.

Around this time, Hinduism of the Vedas, that had been composed a thousand years before the birth of Gautama, was going through many changes. The fire sacrifices of the Vedas were meant for tribal and nomadic societies. As people became more urban, the sacrifices became more elaborate. These rituals made some people unhappy. The other path shown by Mahavira was the one of extreme self-discipline. Buddhism showed a path neither as ritualistic as Hinduism nor as austere as Jainism, and this middle path attracted people.

The Buddha wandered through North India spreading his ideas. People liked his philosophy since it was open to all. It did not need one to perform rituals, or to engage a priest. The paintings in Ajanta show many foreigners – Egyptians, Ethiopians, Greeks, Romans, Persians and Parthians. Had the Buddha's philosophy reached them and their respective countries too? We do not know about the others but Pyrrho of Elis, a Greek poet in Alexander's army did take back Buddhist ideas. What we do know next is from the time of Ashoka. After the war of Kalinga, the Mauryan king was so disgusted with the trail of death that he had brought about that he turned to Buddhism. He is credited with spreading the ideas of Buddhism far and wide through the first inscribed 'broadcasts' which came to be called Ashoka's Rock Edicts (turn to page 149). It was Ashoka who commissioned experts to find out more about the events of the Buddha's life. He sent missionaries to different countries to spread Buddhism. They went to Burma and Suvarnabhumi in the south, to Central Asia in the north, to the Greek states in the northwest and to Ceylon in the south. He had royal roads improved in all directions so that communication could become better.

After the time of Ashoka, missionaries and monks continued to spread the Buddha's teachings all the way to China and Japan. Surprisingly, the religion that believes in simple living was also spread by wealthy merchants as they travelled all over the world. As in any religion, there were Buddhists with slightly different views. This gave rise to different sects of Buddhism. Like all religions, the common message is of peace and non-violence.

Ahimsa: The Power of Non-Violence

Knocking down your classmate to get ahead in the race is a violent act. But *thinking* of knocking down the class bully who always wants to be ahead? That's also a violent act. Yes, not fair, right? Non-violence, in most religions, means not doing harm knowingly or unknowingly, by word, action or thought to another living thing. Non-violence is preached and practised by peace-loving people all over the world. And yet, most people associate the word 'non-violence' or 'ahimsa' with India and also with Mahatma Gandhi. How did this association come about?

Long before Mahatma Gandhi used the power of non-violence to make the British leave India, ahimsa – not doing harm – was very much part of the Yoga Sutra (you'll find more about that on page 196).

Russian author Leo Tolstoy was a great believer in non-violence. He wrote a series of letters to a young Gandhi. Tolstoy's thoughts influenced him in a big way, leading him to use non-violent protest as a way to make the British see the truth – that Indian needed self-rule. Not everyone agreed with his idea. But he persisted. His views on non-violence spread throughout the world. Among the many who were influenced by his call for ahimsa were Martin Luther King Jr who fought (with words, not with guns!) for the rights of African-Americans in America, Nelson Mandela who worked for people's rights in South Africa and Khan Abdul Ghaffar Khan who often spoke about how non-violence was a part of the Quran, Islam's holy book.

BUTTONS

Buttons are cute and colourful and bright and beautiful and all that. They are also a pain when one goes missing in your school shirt and a hawk-eyed monitor or teacher catches you. At such times, you may be excused for crying out (in your mind, of course), 'Who invented buttons!' The people who invented them cannot stand up because, well, they lived in the IVC, more than 4,000 years ago.

The earliest button-like artefacts have been discovered in various sites of the IVC, like Mohenjo-daro. These were made with curved seashells. Some had holes, some did not have holes, and many researchers believe these were used more to beautify a garment than to fasten an opening in it. Later excavations brought up buttons made of shell, bone and clay. These too could have been only decorative, or may have been functional. Archaeologists also found what are called button seals – button-sized clay tablets with a pattern or script on them – used to print a mark. Unlike buttons, these were probably used as 'identity cards' or 'passports'. The IVC included many cities. It is believed that people of each city carried a seal connecting their origin to a particular city.

The idea of buttons as an adornment could have travelled to other parts of the world through trade, and exchange of cultures through travellers. In ancient Rome, between the 1st century BCE and 5th century CE, people flaunted buttons made of bone, wood and metal, with gold and silver work on them. As status symbols, buttons became so important that, around 1250 CE, a button-making guild was set up in Paris. It was open to apprentices, but they had to pay one-fifth of their earnings as button-makers to the guild, and one-tenth of their earnings to the king. (If you feel like doing a bit of maths, find out what fraction was left for the poor apprentice.)

The history of button-making is hazy in India after the decline of the IVC. In 1905, a sub-inspector of schools, Bhulawan Lal, started handcrafting buttons from oyster shells that he found in the Sikrahna River. In 1908, one of India's first button factories was set up in his small town, Mehsi, in East Champaran district, Bihar. Called Tirhut Moon Button Factory, it made buttons out of oyster shells which became a rage with French fashion houses.

Over the years, it has become illegal to use the shells of protected species of sea animals. When ivory became expensive and later illegal to trade, button makers of the world started using 'vegetable ivory', or the nut of the tagua palm.

Many people like to collect buttons, and they are called button collectors or buttoners. Some of you may think that it is pointless. Just like the buttons on the underside of the sleeves on some jackets!

CALICO

Can you guess the state cat of Maryland in the United States of America? The calico cat! They chose this cat because its tricolour coat of black, white and orange is close to the colours of the state flag, the state bird, Baltimore Oriole, and state insect, Baltimore Checkerspot Butterfly. Now, let's see how these cats in the USA got their name from a cloth first made in Calicut (now Kozhikode) in Kerala.

Calico is a coarse cloth woven with unbleached and unrefined cotton. The roughness may come from the pieces of husk and seeds in the cloth. In the 11th century, calico cloth was woven in Calicut. The cloth was printed with small patterns in bright colours. The demand for the cloth rose. Printed calico was quite a useful material. Traders took it from India to Cairo (in present-day Egypt), the capital of the Ottoman Empire at that time. That was why a piece of calico printed in Gujarat was found in Egypt.

England in the 18th century was proud of its woollen and worsted cloth (or textile made out of fine woollen yarn). The East India Company had started importing printed calico from India. To ensure that England's woollens did not lose their market, the first Calico Laws were passed in 1700 to prevent the trade of printed or dyed calico from

India, China or Persia. Since unbleached plain calico was allowed to be exported, these countries began to make grey calico, which was imported by England and printed there with their own patterns.

In the 1800s, England started importing cotton from America and, with machines of their own, they started manufacturing fine printed calico. This caused the decline of calico in India. Calico is still used in India, mostly as practice cloth. Designers working on new cuts use this comparatively inexpensive material to try out their ideas. While calico moved across continents, the textile is still made in Gujarat and on the Malabar Coast. Samples of the old calicos have been preserved in the Calico Museum of Textiles, curated by the Sarabhai Foundation in Ahmedabad.

What's in a Name?

What do an aster flower in North America, the shubunkin goldfish in Japan and a particular potato salad have in common? They're all colourful and are prefixed with 'calico'!

CARDAMOM

It is used in chewing gum, gulab jamun, Finnish cakes, Swedish pastries, Chinese tea and Bedouin coffee. Cardamom, 'the queen of spices', is the third most expensive spice in the world after saffron and vanilla. Ancient Indians may have known it since at least 3000 BCE.

Cardamom grew wild in the Western Ghats and is native to India and Sri Lanka. The southern stretch of the Ghats is called Cardamom Hills or Yela Mala because its terrain and climate allow for the best growth of cardamom plants. Indians were the first to start harvesting and exporting wild cardamom. Plantations were established in the beginning of the 19th century, as under-crops in coffee and pepper plantations. The British established plantations in Coorg (now Kodagu), Chikkamagaluru, Sakleshpur, Valparai and Wayanad, all in the Western Ghats and in the Shevaroy Hills in the Eastern Ghats.

No two spices may be more dissimilar in taste than ginger and cardamom, but they both belong to the same botanical family called *Zingiberaceae* and are both used to make masala chai! *Elettaria cardamomum* gets its scientific name from *elam*, as the spice is called in Sanskrit, Malayalam, Tamil, Telugu and Kannada and the Greek word for 'spice plant', *kardamomon*. The other spice, black cardamom or big cardamom, is also from the same family but has a different taste with the scientific name *Amomum subulatum*. This is grown widely in Nepal and northeast India.

The earliest mention of cardamom has been found in the Ayurvedic texts *Sushruta Samhita* and *Charaka Samhita*. It was also known in Sumer, the earliest civilization in the southern part of the land that later came to be called Mesopotamia. In fact, Indian spices like cardamom and turmeric were cultivated in the gardens of Babylon even as far back as the 8th century BCE. King Ashurbanipal of Assyria (668 BCE–633 BCE) had a scroll made in cuneiform writing that recorded a long list of aromatic plants including cardamom. India exported large quantities of the spice through ancient trade routes to Egypt and Greece. Here, they were used in perfumes and in medicines. The Romans got a whiff of the spice and started adding it to their food. Greek physician and author of *De Materia Medica*, Dioscorides (40 CE–90 CE), makes a mention of cardamom in his work. So booming was the trade that it became one of the dutiable items at the port of Alexandria by 176 CE.

While cardamom cultivation continued in Sri Lanka and other regions in South Asia, India continued to be the largest producer and exporter of cardamom.

Across the world, but almost along the same latitude, a political change was happening in Guatemala in the 1880s. For long under Spanish control, even after the country gained independence, the indigenous people were not given the respect they deserved. The government invited immigrants to take the community's Mayan land and establish coffee and sugarcane plantations. In 1914, a German plantation owner Carl Oskar Majus Klöffer used this scheme to cultivate cardamom on his land with seeds brought from Kerala. The experiment was a success and cardamom started being grown widely in the cloud forests of Guatemala. Today, this country is the largest producer and exporter of cardamom, putting India in second place. The other cardamom-growing countries are Cambodia, El Salvador, Laos, Papua New Guinea, Sri Lanka and Vietnam.

The next time you're asked to pound a few seeds of cardamom to add to the kheer, think about its wild journey from India to the world.

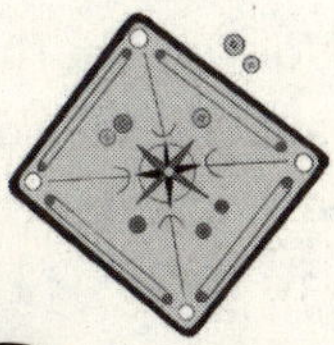

CARROM

On a cold August afternoon in Antarctica, what would researchers do to beat the polar blues? Play carrom! When researchers need a break from their work on atmospheric, earth, chemical and medical sciences, they play carrom, sing, dance and even make a film, like the one made at the base, Bharati Station, for the Winter International Film Festival of Antarctica.

While it is not known who invented the game or when exactly, carrom is believed to have originated in India in the 18th century. There are some people who believe that the Portuguese brought it to India or that similar games existed in ancient Egypt and Burma but there is no proof yet of these beginnings. There is also no proof for the claim that carrom came out of billiards, though some people do call the game 'finger billiards'.

Carrom is a much-loved indoor game that can be played by two people, or by four. It involves a square wooden board on which nine white, nine black and one red (the queen) discs called coins or carrom-men are placed. Players use a striker, a larger and stronger disc, to flick the coins in such a way that they land in the holes at each corner. Maharajas and maharanis may have played it, and so have our families for many generations. No wonder, the game has featured in several popular films. Have you seen one featuring the game?

The game may have travelled the world either with the visitors who came to India or through Indian settlers abroad. Nearly 75 countries play the game that started in the Indian subcontinent. It has remained popular in many Asian countries including India, Sri Lanka, Pakistan, Afghanistan, Nepal, Bangladesh, Malaysia, Maldives, the United Arab Emirates, Japan and Korea. In Europe, strikers send the carrom-men caroming (the verb, meaning to hit a surface and come off it at a different angle) in many countries including Austria, Belgium, France, Germany, Greece, Italy, Poland, Portugal, Spain, Switzerland and the United Kingdom.

India makes and exports carrom boards. Most of them are made in Meerut, Uttar Pradesh. During the Partition, many families of artisans are believed to have moved from Sialkot, in present-day Pakistan, to Meerut. Here, artisans often fit together plywood from Bengal, kikar or babul wood frames from Rajasthan, back support from Hapur, Uttar Pradesh, and pockets crocheted by women of Tejgarhi, Uttar Pradesh. From here, the boards go all over the world, including to Canada and the United States of America.

Winning at carrom requires concentration, sharp eyes and fingers that are nimble, strong and steady. But as a non-competitive game, it is fun. It can also be played solo and is a great way to discharge pent up energy and emotions. Try it next time you're feeling frustrated with something.

CASHMERE

Do you know that feeling when your elbow is itching, and you can't stop scratching it through the day? The condition is called pruritus, and could be caused by dry weather, or an allergy to a soap or something you ate, or an insect bite or your brand-new school sweater.

People have used natural fibres like wool for hundreds of years to make sweaters and coats. Cashmere is one such fibre, made from the soft undercoat of the cashmere goats, which are found mostly in Mongolia, China, Afghanistan, Iran and also in the Himalayan regions of India. The goats in this cold region have double-fleece, with the outer coat made up of coarser and longer strands, and the inner one made up of extremely fine and soft strands. How many strands of the under fleece would you have to bundle to get a strand as thick as a human hair? At least four to six!

While we are looking at numbers, here are some more. One goat can yield about 100 gm of wool each year, and at least 500 gm is needed to make one sweater. A cashmere sweater can keep you eight times warmer than a sheep wool sweater. After all, cashmere goats survive in temperatures as low as minus 40 degrees centigrade!

During spring and summer, the goats start shedding their winter coat, and the goatherders gather or comb out the fibre to make it into yarn. Craftspersons in the Kashmir region are the most adept at processing this fleece and weaving it into different forms, thereby lending their name to this wool. Cashmere yarn as well as scarves and shawls were traded as early as the 3rd century CE on ancient trade routes. The Europeans fell in love with the softness of this material and the demand for it grew. The rich and famous showed off their cashmere scarves at gatherings. Napoleon Bonaparte, the Corsican-born French general, once gifted cashmere shawls to his wife Josephine. She liked them so much that she wore them often, making it a rage in Europe.

In the 19th century, when British officers went back from India, they would carry cashmere shawls and scarves as gifts. They gave the name 'cashmere' to this soft material, an anglicized form of Kashmir.

Cashmere sweaters are also hypoallergenic – they do not contain a chemical called lanolin found in sheep wool, which may cause allergies. Plus, cashmere is light and breathable; depending on the humidity of the air, it either absorbs or releases water vapour, to keep you warm or cool.

So, should you ask for a cashmere sweater for yourself? No, please, not unless you're very rich and can afford to buy it from ethical manufacturers. And not if you love animals. You see, while cashmere wool used to be gathered gently from goats that grazed in large grasslands, the wool is now combed out more violently. Goats are reared in smaller areas for this purpose. Many manufacturers mix other cheaper strands like acrylic to bring down the cost of the clothes. And that may be the reason why some sweaters make you itchy.

Cheque

During the Mauryan period (that is roughly between 321 BCE–185 BCE), a very important development took place – the birth of a financial system of cheques. It was called an *adesha*, 'an order to pay'. If A had to give B a certain amount of money – could be gold, or silver, or coins – and he had the money in a bank or with a banker, A would give B an *adesha* instead of the money. B would take the *adesha* to the banker, and the banker would pay the specified amount to B.

The Mauryan Empire used coins made of silver and copper. The roughly beaten coins were cut in different shapes, with punch marks to show the different denominations. The coins were called *pana*, *ardha-pana*, *pada* and *asta-bhaga* or *ardhapadika*. Instead of carrying a lot of coins, and running the risk of being robbed, people started using *adesha* or 'an order to pay' the bearer.

Since this was over 2,200 years ago, the cheques were not made of paper. The orders may have been engraved on thin strips of metal. The Mauryans had an extensive trade route beyond their kingdom. A few centuries later, Ancient Romans used a similar banking instrument called *praescriptiones* in the 1st century BCE. By the 3rd century CE, the people in the Persian world had started issuing a letter of credit called *chak* (a legal or money-related document), which became *sakk* in the Arabic-speaking countries.

In the 16th century, merchants in bigger cities and in international trading centres like Holland began using 'bills of exchange' or 'letters of credit'. The first recorded use of a hand-written cheque (which later came to be spelled cheque in England, check in America) in Britain was in 1659. By 1717, the Bank of England had gone one step further by keeping forms printed on special cheque paper, the first of modern cheques. In India, the first known printed cheque was used in 1770 by the Bank of Hindustan, founded by a group of Armenian and British merchants in Calcutta.

While the use of cheques has declined drastically after the popularity and ease of digital payments, they are still in use. A standard cheque has six important elements – the drawee (the bank that will pay the money, pre-printed), the date on which the cheque has been written, the payee (to whom the money is paid), the amount to be paid (in numbers and words), the signature of the drawer (the person who is paying the amount) and machine-readable account information (pre-printed).

One of the biggest financial frauds used to be that of bounced cheques. Fraudsters write out a cheque to a person. When the person presents the cheque at the bank, he finds out that the fraudster does not have that amount in the bank.

There is still one cheque we see very often. Guess? Yes, the symbolic cheques that are given at public events to winners, like at a cricket match.

CHESS

How do you make a topic an enjoyable one? Some people make it into a game. Gamification is the process of using the fun elements of games, like winning against a friendly opponent, scoring points and following rules to make other subjects or activities easier to follow. You may have played games that help you understand mathematics and science and history better. Our ancestors were doing this when they invented games to help teach royal pupils how to run their kingdoms. Chaturanga was one such game.

Chaturanga literally means ‘four limbs’ in Sanskrit. The four arms represented the four sections of the army at that time – soldiers on foot, on horses, on elephants and in chariots. It was a game that helped young princes and princesses learn the art of military strategy. The modern game of chess evolved from this ancient game of chaturanga that was invented during the Gupta dynasty in 6th century CE. The game may have been played in some form even earlier because there is a mention of it in the *Arthashastra* written during the Mauryan period. That is some five hundred years before the beginning of the Gupta period. Chaturanga is seen by many as the common ancestor of many chess-like war-games, like *xiangji* (China), *janggi* (Korea), *makruk* (Siam, now Thailand) and *sittuyin* (Myanmar), and *shogi* (Japan).

The idea for the game may have come from even further back in history, from the time of the Indus Valley Civilization. Archaeologists have found remains of dice (some people believe chess was once started with the roll of a dice), game pieces and game boards in several IVC sites. Some of them resemble today's chess boards. How those led to chaturanga though is not yet clear. A game of chaturanga ended when the rajah was removed from the board. When the game moved towards Persia, the rajah was replaced with a shah. Chaturanga became *chatrang* in Persian, *shatranj* in Arabic. The end of the game was announced with a whoop of '*Shah mat*!', meaning the 'shah is helpless', and when the game moved further, the Russians called it *shakmati*. Then it became popular in Europe around 1000 CE. Here, the rules started changing. In Latin, the game was seen not as the killing of the king but as a series of checks to stop the advancement. Latin '*scacchi*' for checks became *échecs* in French, from where it became chess in English.

According to some books, like historian Ibn Khallikan's *Biographical Dictionary*, originally written in Arabic, the game of chess was invented by the Indian Sissa ibn Dahir for the amusement of the King Shihram. The king was so impressed by the game that he said to Sissa, 'Ask me for whatever you desire.' Sissa asked for wheat grains – one on the first square, two on the second, and that the number be progressively doubled on each square. The king found out that the number grew so big and so fast, that there were not enough grains of wheat in the entire world to make up that quantity!

The beauty of the game inspired poets, painters and sculptors. Indian artisans carved out beautiful chess pieces in wood and ivory. Chess is now played in over 170 countries. The oldest governing body of chess was started in Paris, France, over hundred years ago and is called the Fédération Internationale des Échecs (FIDE). It is now headquartered in Lausanne, Switzerland. India has had many grandmasters, 94 when counted in March 2026 including Viswanathan Anand (who was the champion in 2007, 2008, 2010, 2012) and Mayank Chakraborty (2026).

CHUTNEY

Spicy, bland, red, green, tasty, runny, thick, sweet or sour, if it is a finger-licking good accompaniment to a dish, it could be a chutney. This everyday dish in most Indian homes may have got its name from the Hindustani word 'chaatna' (to lick), implying something that can be scooped with your fingers and licked with relish. Served in small portions, it is supposed to last the entire course of an Indian lunch, with a lick of it at intervals. Even with several dishes on your plate, the tongue and mind may be missing some elements; a good chutney is such a mix of micronutrients, and a burst of flavours, that just a lick of it makes the food so much more satisfying.

But what is chutney? It is a bit difficult to define this, but at the risk of being beaten into pulp or chutney by someone who disagrees, a chutney is a preparation made by pounding or grinding together pieces of fruit, vegetable or nut along with spices to make it a sharp-tasting condiment. It may be made with fresh, uncooked ingredients or with cooked ingredients like sautéed tomato, brinjal or Indian borage, coarsely or finely ground, runny or almost dry, with the addition of green or red chillies and a sour ingredient like tamarind or lemon juice. There are hundreds of variations possible. Food writer Krish Ashok came up with an algorithm called the Amaklamatic Chutney Generator Matrix (*amakalam* means fantastic in Tamil) to help home cooks improvise chutneys without following a specific recipe. In some parts of central India, red ant chutney is quite popular, and in Bengal, there is something called plastic chutney. Totally edible, and biodegradable, it is made with slices of raw papaya that are translucent and bright like clear plastic!

Chutney is one of the oldest prepared foods of India. While there are some reports that say Indians may have been licking their chutney-fingers way before 500 BCE, we do not yet have proof of that. It is, however, mentioned in the Jain literature written between 7th and 14th century CE. Later, the hakims of the Mughal rulers in India are supposed to have introduced ingredients like dates to the mix.

Spicy mango chutneys were in demand. But, since not all of the British folks could take the heat, they started adding sugar, making it almost a jam. Fruit chutneys in pretty ceramic jars became a popular thing to gift as luxury items. These came to be called mangoed fruits! The colonial British took these chutneys to their other colonies, including those in the Caribbean and also back to Britain.

Every region of India has a different variation of chutney depending on the local produce. Many regional medicinal plants go into the making of a local chutney. Just like the chutney travelled from India to the world, so did its music. Trinidad and Tobago, the island country close to South America, has a genre of music called chutney music. Why? Because it is a mix of several kinds of music coming from Hindustani folk music, Bhojpuri folk music and Caribbean calypso!

James Bond's Indian Connection

Whether you've seen a James Bond movie or not, you must be familiar with the opening shot of James Bond with his gun and the theme music, right? The character was created by British author Ian Fleming in 1952 for the book *Casino Royale*. The music was composed by British musicians Monty Norman and John Barry. But where did the theme music come from? From India! Well, sort of. You see, Norman and Barry composed the tune for a musical based on the book *A House for Mr Biswas*, written by Trinidad-born Nobel laureate V.S. Naipaul. Since the story is set in an Indian community in Trinidad, the composers used many Indian instruments. But the musical was never completed. When they had to compose music for the James Bond film *Dr. No* in 1962, they reused the music. And that became the most iconic film theme music ever!

COCONUT

No, the coconut palm probably did not originate in India. And no, India is not the largest producer or exporter of coconut even though the Syrian Greek traveller and merchant, Cosmas Indicopleustes (the Traveller of the Indies), called it the 'Great Nut of India' in his book *Topographia Christiana.* Ctesias, a Greek historian, author and physician to the Persian king, had mentioned 'coconut fruits' in passing a thousand years before him. But, according to scientific studies, the southern margin of the Indian subcontinent is a secondary centre of origin of coconut *Cocos nucifera.* Called the Indo-Atlantic region, it was one of the two regions of the origin of cultivation of coconuts.

The most popular belief is that *Cocos nucifera* originated somewhere in the area called Malesia (Not Malaysia!), roughly covering the biological regions of present-day Southeast Asia, Indonesia, New Guinea and some Pacific Islands, and that it was introduced to India some 2,500 years back by Austronesians. The other theory is that coconuts fell into oceans and found their own shores all over the world. Capable of staying afloat and safe for months together, they reached different shores of the tropical world and put down their roots. Some of them also reached the southwest coasts of India. It was here that they began to be cultivated.

How old is the coconut? Researchers believe it existed 20 million years ago, long before humans evolved on this planet. While it is not the magical, wish-fulfilling *Kalpavriksha* mentioned in the *Samudra Manthan* story, the coconut palm is one of the many trees called the *Kalpavriksha* in some parts of the country because it fulfils the wish of having '*roti, kapda aur makaan*' (a popular phrase in Hindi), plus *gaadi*! It is so versatile that one can survive on it – you can eat the white inner part, drink the water, use the husk to start a fire or to make rope, weave the leaf fronds to make a roof and cut the trunk to build rafts, or a home.

Coconuts are not mentioned in the Vedas even though coconuts have been a part of India's religious rites for ages. But they do roll into the Ramayana, the Mahabharata, the Upanishads and the Jataka Tales, all composed after the Vedic period. Chinese pilgrim Xuanzang who visited India in 640 CE mentions coconuts in Assam. Persian geographer Ibn Khurdadhbih, in his book *Kitab al-Masalik wa al-Mamalik* (*The Book of Roads and Kingdoms*) written in the 9th century mentions coconut as one of the commodities imported from India.

The mystery around the origin of the coconut continues. With India being a progressive and busy trading hub, coconuts, like many other commodities, were introduced to different countries. In the 15th century, when the Portuguese had taken over parts of India's coasts, they filled up available space on their ships with coconuts – even though they much preferred the more lucrative spices to the hard nut – which by the way is botanically not even a nut but a fruit!

Nuts about Rugby

Where in the world is rugby played with a well-oiled coconut? Manipur! The game is called Yubi Lakpi, literally meaning 'coconut snatching'. (Which international game is Manipur famous for? Find out on page 134.)

COTTON CULTIVATION

Cotton was discovered by different regions of the world, independent of each other. Wild cotton came as a different species. Of the four species that were first domesticated, *Gossypium arboreum* L. was cultivated in the Indus Valley of Pakistan and India. The others were grown between Arabia and Syria, in Mesoamerica and in South America. Wild cotton was discovered and used at least 6,000 years ago in the Indus Valley. The earliest archaeological evidence of this was found in Mehrgarh. (Where is this? Look it up on page 24) Cultivation started later, maybe around 3000 BCE.

Cities like Mohenjo-daro flourished because of trade in cotton, among other things. Raw cotton and cloth were exported to Dhuweila in Jordon, and further to Maikop, in present-day Russia. It was even cultivated briefly in the Assyrian botanical gardens of Nineveh, in present-day Iraq. But cotton being a tropical plant was difficult to grow outside the Indian subcontinent. Only thousands of years later did cultivation begin slowly in other places such as in the Persian Gulf, North Africa and Uzbekistan. The plant was introduced to China only in the first millennium CE, that too as an ornamental plant. If you've seen a cotton plant, you know how beautiful it is – delicate yellow flowers, that give rise to hard bolls, that crack open to let the cotton pop out in a cloud. Between 900–1000 CE, cotton cultivation spread fast into Southwest Asia, North Africa, Persia and the Mediterranean regions.

The word 'cotton' comes from the Arabic term *al-qutun*, which became *algodón* in Spanish and cotton in English. Greek historian and writer Herodotus (c. 450 BCE) was referring to India when he wrote about '...wild trees there which produce wool as their fruit'. Visitors to ancient India marvelled at the cotton produced here. Marco Polo who visited India in the 13th century, wrote about the fine cotton of Masulipatam (now Machilipatnam, in Andhra Pradesh), '...here are made the most beautiful and valuable cotton cloths in the world; also the thinnest and most delicate, resembling our spiders' webs'. He also spoke highly of the cottons from other parts of India.

India's art showed in its cotton weaves. Cotton material was traded heavily, reaching Indonesia and Japan in the east, and Egypt, Arabia and Ethiopia in the west. The Japanese learnt that the fabulous European-cut clothes worn by Portuguese merchants in the 16th century were made with India's calico (what's that? Turn to page 36) and chintz. The fabrics were soon made into, guess what? Kimonos, of course!

A Dutch spy, traveller and trader, Jan Huyghen van Linschoten, in his The Voyage of John Huyghen van Linschoten to the East Indies (1598), wrote about the 'excellent faire linnen of Cotton...' and the 'cunning workmanship' of the weavers. Indian cotton was grown with indigenous seeds, and the entire community was involved in growing, harvesting, spinning and weaving cotton. This made production healthy and sustainable. Up to the 17th century, only native seeds were used. Later, many other seeds were brought in, either deliberately or by mistake.

When the demand for Indian cloth boomed, European traders took over the trade. Production had to increase. During the British rule in India, industrialized weaving began in England. Farmers were made to switch to foreign seeds that would produce cotton strong enough for machines. The seeds were expensive. Not only was the biodiversity of Indian cotton damaged, but foreign seeds also brought in over 160 varieties of pests!

The Money Plant (Literally!)

That cotton brought ancient Indians a lot of wealth is known. But do you know that cotton also literally makes up money, well, currency? Indian notes are made with 100 per cent cotton fibre, not wood-based paper. That's probably why the forgotten note in your pocket comes back untorn even after it has been wringed in a washing machine!

CUCUMBER

Cucumber is one of the coolest fruits known to us. Yes, it is botanically a fruit because we eat the part that comes from the flower and has seeds. But let's continue calling it a green vegetable so that we can tick off at least one vegetable that most of us like. Why is it cool? Because raw cucumber is 95 per cent water. Eating it hydrates the body.

Cucumber (*Cucumis sativus*) originated in the foothills of the Himalayas in India and Nepal. It belongs to the family *Cucurbitaceae*, just like melons. The original cucumbers were extremely bitter. Selective breeding and cultivation, which was done in India for at least 3,000 years is what made cucumber such a cool snack. The seeds were taken to China where they were cultivated for at least 2,000 years. Cucumbers grow on vines.

Cucumber seeds travelled through land routes and sea routes, and cultivation began in Iran, Iraq and Turkey during the 6th–7th centuries. Cultivation began in Spain in the 9th century, and in Tunisia in the 10th century. Christopher Colombus is said to have carried cucumber seeds from the Canary Islands in Spain to Hispaniola in the Caribbean in the late 15th century, thus introducing cucumbers to the Americas. Many centuries later, pickled gherkins – a small variety of cucumbers – became very popular in the USA after a ketchup company put it on its product list.

Not all cucumbers taste good. Some with warty skin can be quite bitter. Between the 16th to 19th centuries, the people of Great Britain started distrusting uncooked food, especially the cucumbers with thick skin. They nicknamed this humble fruit 'cowcumber' because they thought it was fit only for cows to eat. Not cool, right? However, it was the 18th century British poet John Gay who gave us the phrase 'cool as a cucumber' by including it in his comic ballad 'A New Song of New Similes'.

Whether you like them as slices or in *kachumber*, *kosambari*, *singju* or raita, or cooked in *akki* rotis or *gojju*, cucumbers are good for you. One of the best things to snack on when you feel a bit low on energy is a bit of cucumber.

Some Cool Applications

A slice of cucumber pressed to the roof of your mouth for 30–90 seconds is supposed to freshen your breath. (No, it won't kill the bacteria that causes bad breath; only a dentist can solve that problem.)

Noisy hinges? Rub a slice of cucumber on them.

Want to keep lizards away from a specific place like a counter or dining table? Keep a slice of cucumber or cucumber peels there. (But of course, these may attract fruit flies!)

Have a sunburn? Rub a slice of cucumber on the skin.

Tired eyes? Sit back with two slices over the eyes. (That means, you automatically are off screens too, that may have caused tiredness.)

CURRY

What is curry? It has many correct answers. In south India, where the word came from, *kari* could mean a dry dish of sautéed vegetables, or a spicy dish of mutton, chicken and vegetables cooked in a gravy. Both are eaten with rice. '*Kari*' literally means black or blackened, and that is why coal is also called kari in Tamil. (Have you read the delightful tale of *Kari the Elephant* by Dhan Gopal Mukerji? Guess the colour of this elephant?)

Or, curry may have meant a dish spiced with black pepper. The rest of India hardly uses the word! Bengal has *jhol*, Gujarat has *undhiyu*, the Telugu-speaking region has *kura*, Lakshadweep has *mus kavaab* and Kashmir has *haak saag* with rice. There's the Mughlai *kurma* and the Parsi *sali boti*. All these dishes would be called curry by someone new to India's regional cuisine. There are a hundred different dishes in India that a non-Indian would call curry.

So how did curry become one of the most popular Indian dishes in, say, London or Chicago? Let's start with the Portuguese who came to India and settled down here for a really long time by colonizing parts of the country. During their spice trade along the Coromandel Coast, they came across a spice blend called *kari podi*. This spice mix made it to a cookery book written in Portuguese published in the 17th century. In Goa, when they saw a dish that locals ate with rice, they called it *caril*. In Portuguese, the plural of the word would be *carie*. In English, it became curry. The British took a liking to local dishes, but it was too much of a task to remember each dish. So, they called all of them – that went on rice, or with rotis – curry. But they couldn't take the heat of the spices. So, curry powders labelled Mild, Medium and Hot were sold.

Anglo-Indian cuisine gained popularity. Hannah Glasse in her 1747 book *The Art of Cookery Made Plain and Easy* gives recipes for 'currey', where the spices used are 'turmerick', pepper and ginger. The book helped curry to reach England and the many colonies of the British around the world. A spice mix that came to be called Madras curry powder became popular in England and is believed to have found a place in the palace kitchen. Curry powder became a luxury item that made it to the list in the *South-Carolina and American General Gazette* in 1771.

While other countries in Asia have their own recipes, also called curry, including Japan's *kare raisu*, the Western world has made curry an umbrella term for the dishes that we usually eat with rice, or roti.

The Leaf in the Curry

Curry does not get its name from the curry leaves that may go into some curries. These dark (and, therefore, the name *kari* or black in South Indian languages), aromatic leaves are packed with goodness. No wonder they are used to make chutneys, pickles and to garnish many curries. While the leaves of the *Bergera koenigii* tree are also used in Ayurvedic preparations, in Queensland, Australia, the plant is categorized as a weed.

If you want butterflies to visit your garden, plant a curry tree. It makes a perfect host plant for the *Papilio polytes* or Common Mormon, a beautiful swallowtail butterfly.

DECIMAL SYSTEM

A window is a window is a window, right? Or, is it? What happens when you put a window right at the base of a wall? It becomes a door for a pet cat or dog. Place a window in the ceiling and you get a skylight. Place it high up in a wall and it becomes a ventilator or an exhaust. In mathematics, a digit is a digit is a digit? Let's see. The first 2 in 2026 indicates 2000, and the second 2 indicates 20. Placing is everything! The value of a digit changes depending on where you place it. This place value system became possible when the ancient Indians hit upon the idea of a base-10 system, first with just a dot to indicate 'nothing' and later with the invention of the revolutionary zero.

You may already have read about the nine symbols and how they spread to the world (on page 4). The tenth symbol is at the end of the book since it is spelt with a 'z'. The numerals 0–9 make up a decimal system. Decimal comes from the Old Latin word *decem* for 'ten', and *decimus* for 'tenth' and was used in English only in the early 1600s. Some people also say it may have come from the Sanskrit *dasa* that means 'ten'. There is no concrete proof that the first written evidence of the decimal system appears in a copper plate in Gujarat or in an inscription in a temple in Gwalior, but the *Yoga Sutra* (check this out on page 196) by Patanjali dated 150 CE does mention the decimal system. The *Aryabhatiya*, a set of 32 Sanskrit verses about astronomy and mathematics, written in the 5th century by 23-year-old Aryabhata, also features the decimal place value system. The decimal system started being used in other Asian countries too. Many of these countries had their own mathematical systems. Along with India's number system, the ancient decimal system spread from India to the rest of the world.

Decimal Currency

There was a time in India when one could get 192 pies for 1 rupee? Surprised? That's because a pie was the smallest unit of currency. 3 pies = 1 pice. 4 pice = 1 anna. 16 annas = 1 rupee. Can you imagine how complicated calculations would have been? Aren't you glad India follows the decimal system since 1 April 1957. Since then, 1 rupee = 100 paise. Simple! For a land that invented the decimal numeral system, India took a really long time to use it in its currency. Russia was the first to convert to decimal currency in 1704. Only two countries still do not follow this currency system, Mauritania in North Africa and Madagascar, the island country in southeast Africa.

DENTISTRY

Skeletal remains in Mehrgarh showed drill holes similar to the ones made for today's root canal treatment. What did the Harappans drill with? Who were the surgeons? How did they learn all this? We do not know this yet.

We do know that Ayurveda has been practised for thousands of years. Ayurveda uses several herbs and preparations for dental care. Neem, mango, babul, miswak and guava twigs are still used as chewing sticks and believed to be good to keep plaque at bay. Ayurvedic preparations are used as antiseptic, antioxidant and analgesic. We do know that the *Sushruta Samhita* and the *Charaka Samhita* are the ancient reference books for all Ayurvedic physicians, and that these were passed on orally for many centuries before being written down. One of the pioneering practitioners of Ayurveda was Sushruta, an authority on anatomy, surgery (*shalya tantra*), beauty and reconstructive surgical treatment, obstetrics and gynaecology, ophthalmology, orthopaedics, traumatology and pharmacology. He not only treated patients, but started paying attention to post-operative care, invented surgical instruments and documented them in the *Sushruta Samhita*. The Samhitas were composed in Sanskrit. They have specific names for different specialists.

A surgeon is mentioned as *salya vaidya* and a physician is called *bhishaka*. But what was a tooth specialist called? Surprisingly, there is no word for dentist in these works, even though there are many details about treatment for problems to do with the mouth, tongue and teeth.

Some of the instruments used to treat tooth-related issues were *kaakamukha svastika* (forcep inspired by a crow's face), *kankamukha svastika* (heron forcep), *sinhmukha svastika* (lion forcep) and *tarkasmukha svastika* (hyena forcep). The surgical instruments invented by Sushruta, included one to remove dental plaque.

With the translation of the Ayurvedic texts, India's medical knowledge, including that of dentistry, spread too. If you want to sink your teeth into a bit about Ayurveda and how it travelled, turn to page 9.

DIAMOND MINING

Diamonds were formed over three billion years ago, some 150–250 km under the Earth's surface. You may have studied in chemistry class that diamonds are nothing but carbon sitting for millions of years under extremely high pressure and temperature. Then, at some point ancient volcanoes blasted them up to levels that became accessible to humans. In the India of the 4th century, people found these shiny stones in the riverbeds and mountain slopes. The rich soon got enamoured by these rocks. This led to the first rush of demand, starting the diamond mining industry.

Kautilya's *Arthashastra* translated into English by R. Shamasastry, mentions diamonds several times. 'That which is big, heavy, hard (*prahárasaham*, tolerant of hitting), regular (*samakóna*), capable of scratching on the surface of vessels (*bhájanalékhi*), refractive of light (*kubrámi*), and brilliant is the best.' Roman writer of the thirty-seven-volume encyclopaedia *Naturalis Historia*, Pliny the Elder mentioned the diamond's brilliance and hardness in the 1st century CE. (Sad fact: He also died while trying to save people when Mount Vesuvius erupted in 79 CE.)

The diamonds mined in India did not come out from deep pits. They were found on riverbeds, and on the banks of the

Mahanadi, in Kosala (now Odisha). Greco-Roman scholar Claudius Ptolemy wrote in the 1st century CE, in his book *Geographia*, about the city of Sambalaka on the left bank of the Manada River, where diamonds were found. The famous dam built near the once diamond-rich area of Sambalpur gets its name from the word *hirakud*, which means 'diamond island'. Kosala also finds a mention as a source of diamonds in Varāhamihira's *Brihat Samhita* of the 6th century.

Much before the 12th century, diamond mining began in the Krishna River. Legends grew. It was believed that the diamonds were found in caves guarded by snakes in the Nallamala Forest. Based on some folklore, diamond seekers used to throw meat into the caves. The gems would stick to the meat, and huge eagles would pick up these pieces and bring them out of the caves. Such stories even appeared in *Sindbad the Sailor*! These diamonds became famous as the Golconda diamonds. Some of the world's most well-known diamonds – the Koh-i-Noor, the Orlov of Russia, the Daria-i-Noor of Iran and the Hope of the USA – all came from this region.

The caravan trade took diamonds from India to places as far as Venice. By the 15th century, the brilliant stone had become fashionable all over Europe. For over a thousand years from the time it was first discovered, India remained the only source of diamonds. In the early 18th century, miners looking for gold along the banks of the Jequitinhonha River in Brazil found diamonds in Arraial do Tijuco. In the beginning, no one in Europe wanted these diamonds. Then, someone had the brilliant idea to name the place Golconda Velha Mines. Business boomed. The village was later renamed Diamantina. India lost its monopoly, and for the next 150 years, Brazil was the diamond king. The next big source – Kimberley in South Africa – was discovered in 1866.

Lab-made diamonds are gaining popularity among people who are conscious about factors like 'blood diamonds' – diamonds that are mined in places controlled by illegitimate forces, and involve violence and unfair practices. Lab-made diamonds shine just as bright as natural diamonds, and if made fairly, using green energy, they are definitely a more ethical choice.

Panna, in Madhya Pradesh, is the place most sought after by diamond hunters. India is one of the largest importers of diamonds, and one of the largest exporters of cut and polished diamonds in the world.

A Trail of Sparkle

In October 2025, a band of robbers made off with priceless jewels in broad daylight from the Louvre, the famous Parisian museum. They could have, but did not take the famous 140-carat Regent Diamond. Why? Did they believe it was cursed? It was discovered in 1698 in the mines of Golconda, then the capital of the Qutb Shahi dynasty. The man who found it hid it in an incision in his leg, and asked a sea captain to help him escape the country. The man was killed. The diamond was cut in London between 1704 and 1706 and acquired by France's Regent Philippe d'Orléans in 1717. It changed crowns over time, and many of the people who wore it met with ghastly ends. During the French Revolution, King Louis XVI and Marie Antoinette were executed. Napoleon Bonaparte who had it encrusted on his sword was banished from France. Diamonds certainly are not for everyone!

DUNGAREES

Some call them overalls, some call them jumpsuits, and some others call them dungarees. The one-piece coverall dress with pants attached to the bib has adjustable straps over the shoulders.

In the 17th century, Dongri was a thriving dockside settlement, in present-day Mumbai. The local weavers made a rough cloth here that they called dungri. The Britishers working for the East India Company anglicized it to dungaree. Close to the coast, Dongri the place, started trading in this rough and tough fabric often made with indigo-dyed yarn. The fabric was mainly used as a sailcloth. Dongri's location made it an important part of the sea route from India, westwards. The British, Arab and Portuguese traders took the material to different parts of the world.

British sailors found that dungri could be used to make work clothes. The dungri clothes did not tear easily. They were comfortable to wear for long hours and many days on the sea, and hardly needed repairs. What a perfect way of using sailcloth, they thought! And that is how the cloth from Dongri was made into dungarees in the machine shops of England.

Dungarees became the standard clothes for miners, dockyard workers and factory workers by the 1700s, not just in England but in America too. When men left to fight during the World Wars, women started wearing dungarees and working in factories. Dungarees became a symbol of women's empowerment and a demonstration of strength.

After the wars, dungarees became fashionable non-work clothes too. Also, any heavy-duty work uniform (even if made with denim instead of dungri) came to be called dungarees. Movie stars and celebrities in Hollywood wore them. Today, we can wear dungarees made in several colours, and in different fittings. Dongri itself became a fully urban part of the city of Mumbai, with its history forgotten.

In 2024, the place that gave dungarees to the world was back in the news with the Maharashtra government deciding to rename Sandhurst Road Station as Dongri Station.

The French Town of Nimes

Where did denim originate? The Wild West of America? Nah! Denim gets its name from *serge de Nîmes*, meaning 'serge from Nîmes' in French. Serge is a type of twill weave characterized by diagonal ridges on the surface. This fabric was made centuries ago in the once-famous textile town of Nîmes in France. It was made of wool or silk. *Serge de Nîmes* was shortened to denim. Big fashion brands made the same twill material using cotton, and fixed rivets to give the world denim jeans. Oh, and the word jeans may have come from Genoa, Italy, where a cotton, linen and wool blend was first made.

EYE SURGERY

Around 600 BCE, there lived a physician called Sushruta in Kashi who was a pioneer in the treatment of several illnesses including surgery. As a teacher, he passed on his knowledge to his students orally; 'Sushruta' literally means 'one who has thoroughly learnt by hearing' in Sanskrit. At some point, his students (who were called *Saushrutas*) compiled his teachings into what came to be called the *Sushruta Samhita*. How he had time to compose something with 184 chapters describing over 1,120 illnesses and 700 medicinal plants after performing surgeries is unimaginable!

Eighteen chapters in the *Sushruta Samhita* are dedicated to 76 different eye problems. They give detailed instructions on how cataract could be treated with a procedure called couching. Instead of taking out the cataract – the cloudy area in the lens of the eye that leads to a decrease in vision of the eye – Sushruta suggested inserting a special needle that he created and pushing down the cloudy part so that it would not impair vision. Sushruta is regarded as the first person to have conducted this form of eye surgery.

Sushruta Samhita was translated into Arabic in the 8th century during the reigns of the caliphs al-Mansur and Haroun al-Rashid of Baghdad (yes, the one who features in

One Thousand and One Nights). Called *Kitab Shah Shun al-Hindi* (aka *Kitab-i-Susrud*), this led the knowledge of ancient medical practices, including that of eye surgery, to spread to other countries.

Modern eye surgeries may or may not have developed from the work of Sushruta, for people from different places and in different times can come up with the same or similar ideas, right?

FIBONACCI SEQUENCE

What does poetry have to do with mathematics? And what do the Vedas have to do with mathematics? And what does mathematics have to do with sunflower seeds and pinecones? Answers, answers! Acharya Pingala wanted them too.

Pingala was a mathematician and poet. He wanted to study the *chanddh* or metre of Sanskrit verses. You may have noticed that it is easier to recite and remember songs and rhymes than it is to remember a paragraph about the laws of nature, right? The Vedas, like many of the Sanskrit texts, were set in verse because they could be learnt and remembered by recitation. Circa 3rd century BCE, Pingala started studying the verses and saw a pattern of the two basic syllables, the *laghu* (short) and the *guru* (heavy). He composed *Chandashastra* that lists his formula for creating all possible combinations of *laghu* and *guru* syllables. Quite by accident he had also discovered the binary system (a system of combinations using just two values) that became the basic language of computer programming thousands of years later! Though he also used the word *shunya*, to mean nothing, he did not quite use it the way Brahmagupta did (head right to page 199 to know more about him and zero).

Not just that, Pingala's work also includes *matrameru*, meaning 'mountain of meters', a series of combinations using the *laghu* and *guru*. Many centuries later, it formed the basis of what came to be called the Fibonacci series – a sequence of numbers where each number is a sum of the previous two numbers (1, 1, 2, 3, 5, 8, 13, 21...). If you start with 0, 1, the next number is 0+1=1, 1+1=2, 1+2=3, 2+3=5 and so on. Since no one probably saw any useful application for this bit of mathematics, it went unnoticed for long. The mathematician Virahanka, circa 700 CE, carried forward the *Chandashastra* and came up with what he called Sankhyankas. Jain monk Hemachandra, circa 1150 CE, did more work on this.

Meanwhile, in faraway Italy, Leonardo of Pisa was born around 1170. As he grew up, he went with his merchant father to Algiers, Africa. Here he came in contact with many Arab mathematicians and learnt about the Hindu-Arabic numbers. Arabic mathematicians had got much of their knowledge at that time from India. Leonardo wrote a book called the *Liber Abaci* (Latin for *The Book of Calculation*). This helped to tell the western world about the Hindu-Arabic numerals. He described the nature of the sequence but did not give it a name, just like how Pingala did not either.

A couple of centuries later, Leonardo da Vinci was born. As he started becoming more famous, people started referring to the older Leonardo as Fibonacci, short for 'filius Bonacci', meaning 'the son of Bonacci'. The pattern of numbers that he learnt about from Arabic teachers, who learnt it from Indian mathematicians, came to be called the Fibonacci sequence.

The Fibonacci sequence is seen in nature a lot. There are many flowers which have 1, 2, 3, 5, 8, 13 or 21 petals. (Very few have 4, 6, 7, 11 or 12 petals!). If you count the number of spiral arrangements of seeds in a pinecone or sunflower, you'll see that it is a Fibonacci number – it may have 21 spirals or 34, or – you get it. Botanically, the arrangements of seeds ensure that all of them get sunlight and rain (or less rain if desired). Not everything in nature follows the Fibonacci pattern. And even though many people claim that the pattern can be seen in the Pyramids of Giza and many seashells, it isn't really so. But the Fibonacci pattern does sound poetic, doesn't it?

GHEE

Bottles of ghee as gifts? Yes, ghee seems to be a rage again, in Europe at least. You can get ghee in lovely little jars now, bubble-wrapped and safe to be transported. But that was not the case in the first and second centuries. Traders carried ghee – or *butyron* as the Romans called it then – from South India to Rome in leather-skin bags! Now, couldn't people outside India just make their own ghee instead? After all, ghee is just butter that is cooked to take away all water content. Why did they not do it? The answer lies in smelly butter.

Freshly churned butter is a delight to lick up. If not refrigerated, it can change taste and become rancid and smelly very quickly. In the hot subcontinent of India, butter would go bad very soon. A wise Indian (we don't know who) found out that one could heat butter to a stage when all the water content evaporated leaving behind a fragrant liquid that could be stored for long. Is ghee the same as clarified butter? Not exactly. Try making ghee yourself with a blob of unsalted butter. Heat it in a small pan over a low flame. Within minutes, the milk solids separate and move down, leaving a clear liquid above. This liquid is clarified butter. If you continue heating, the milk solids turn brown, the house starts smelling festive, and the liquid turns a bit more golden. That liquid is ghee. Switch off the burner. Decant the ghee. Eat up the crunchy residue, with a bit of jaggery.

Indians had the knack of making the perfect ghee, which is why the ghee-lovers of the world preferred to buy it rather than make it themselves. Traders took it to different parts of the world, even though many cultures like Ethiopia in Africa and Middle Eastern countries had their own variations of ghee. Ghee is mentioned in the Rig Veda and the Bhagavad Gita. *Ghrta*, as ghee is known in Sanskrit, comes from the root word *ghr*, meaning 'to sprinkle'. This is the reason why we top our rice and rotis with a little bit of this healthy fat. Ayurveda lists it as something that can be eaten every day, and believes that ghee is a good source of energy and acts to improve memory and intelligence. It is believed that ghee has a warming effect on our body which explains why winter foods like *gajar ka halwa*, *pongal* and *urad dal halwa* are made with generous amounts of ghee. Of course, just because ghee is a great source of energy and is rich in antioxidants and vitamins A, D, E and K does not mean we can guzzle it.

Ghee is widely used as a cosmetic and medicine. When kids develop chapped lips in India, a parent or grandparent applies some ghee on the lips. When you bite your lip or inner cheek by mistake, what do you do? Apply a bit of ghee on the wound. In Ayurveda, many recipes for its preventive and curative preparations include ghee. Ghee is now a much sought-after ingredient worldwide, with people using it on their skin and hair to make them healthy. Some people even put it in their coffee! Yes, there was a craze in the West called bulletproof coffee, a high-calorie beverage. It involves brewing ghee or butter made with milk from grass-fed cows.

Born 'from the fire', ghee is considered a sacred fat and has been used during religious rituals. Not surprisingly, India is the largest producer of ghee in the world. It is the largest consumer too and exports the highest amount. Ghee made with the milk of different cattle like cow, buffalo, camel or goat have different qualities and importance too. Oh, and even though ghee is a product of lactose-containing milk, it is perfectly safe even for lactose-intolerant people.

HINDUISM

Hinduism is considered the oldest religion in the world. But the word 'Hinduism' itself came into use only a few hundred years ago. The first Indian to have used it may be the reformer Raja Ram Mohan Roy in around 1817. Scholars suggest that more than just one religion, it is an umbrella term to include many different systems of belief, philosophy and ritual.

The early travellers to visit the Indus Valley referred to the people of that area as 'Indoi' in Greek, and 'Hindu' in Persian. 'Hindu' became an exonym for India, that is, a name given by outsiders to a region. By extension, the people of Hindu were called Hindus. Many centuries later, the followers of the Vedic beliefs started calling themselves Hindus and the religion followed by them came to be called Hindu religion. By the 13th century, India also started being called Hindustan, which had nothing to do with religion.

To put it very simply, the core facets of Hinduism include the following. First, the belief in the supreme, universal essence called Brahman. A bit of this essence is in everyone, and everyone is in it. The Brahman may take many forms, and the three most revered forms are that of Brahma the Creator, Vishnu the Preserver and Shiva the Destroyer, (who destroys so that there may be new creation). Second, the concept of reincarnation. Every living being is born in a different form in the next life. Imagine each life as a lump of clay, that can take different shapes. Third, the concept of karma, which says that our actions have reactions. Do good, and your score goes up, do bad, and your score goes down. The results may affect you in the same lifetime or in subsequent births.

The many different systems of the faith started coming together some time in the Vedic age between c. 500 BCE–200 BCE, and 300 CE. Whether the followers believed in one God or many in different forms, and even if one did not believe in God, Hinduism encouraged debate and discussion.

Followers of Hinduism recognize the Vedas, the Upanishads, the Ramayana and the Mahabharata as their sacred texts. Hinduism appealed to many people. It spread to many countries, especially in South Asia. As yoga, the practice of self-realization (which includes asanas), started becoming popular in the West, people also started studying Hinduism. The largest population of Hindus outside India is in Nepal. The next highest Hindu population? In Mauritius! The largest religious structure in the world is Angkor Wat, Cambodia. It was built as a Vishnu temple in the 12th century, but slowly transformed into a Buddhist temple, and is hence called a Hindu-Buddhist temple.

INDIGO CULTIVATION

Indigo is that beautiful colour between violet and blue, as you may know from the rainbow mnemonic VIBGYOR. Your jeans may be indigo, or your hand-dyed Jaipur shirt may be indigo. The colour of these comes from leaves of different plants. The one that yields the most pigment is the *Indigofera tinctoria*, a plant of Indian origin. The leaves of the plant are harvested just before the pretty pink flowers bloom, steeped in water and then fermented. The dye settles down at the bottom of the vat. The best quality indigo was grown and traded in different parts of India – Bayana in Rajasthan, Sarkhej in Gujarat, Agra in Uttar Pradesh and along the Coromandel Coast of south India.

While the earliest evidence of indigo-coloured fabric is from Peru, it has been disputed whether the pigment used was from the plant called woad or from *Indigofera*. The blue stripes on the borders of the linen clothes on Egyptian mummies are dated to around 2400 BCE. Again, the source of the dye cannot be confirmed. The earliest example of *Indigofera* being used for dyeing is from the Indus Valley Civilization. Archaeologists have found remnants of seeds from at least four different species of *Indigofera* from the site in Rojdi in present-day Gujarat.

Remnants of indigo-dyed fabric dated to 1750 BCE were also discovered in Mohenjo-daro.

The colour enchanted the world. Along with Indian spices and gems, indigo dye too was traded heavily. Before the sea routes were found around the Cape of Good Hope to India, merchants carried indigo blocks through the Persian Gulf and then over land to Babylon. Or, they would take it to Arabia, and through the Red Sea to Egypt. From here it would go to Europe. Once the Europeans had found a quicker route to India in the 15th and 16th centuries, trade boomed. The merchants of the East India Company and the Dutch East India Company could not have enough of the dye. Fearing a loss of the sale of the local woad dye, Norway and France banned Indian indigo which they called 'Devil's Dye'.

By the 1700s, cultivation began in other places too. In the French-controlled island of Saint-Domingue (now Haiti), West Africans were enslaved and made to cultivate indigo. It was here that the slaves revolted too and slavery came to an end. In India, the officers of the British rule saw that indigo grew well in Bengal and Bihar. They forced farmers to cultivate indigo instead of food crops. For over 50 years, the farmers bore the burden of cultivating something which earned them very little and put them in huge debt. Can you guess what happened next? Food shortage and famine. In 1859, the farmers of Bengal could take it no more. Nearly five million indigo workers in Bengal went against British orders in a movement that came to be called Neel Bidroha, Bengali for Indigo Revolt.

But indigo cultivation continued. In April 1917, Mahatma Gandhi started the Champaran Satyagraha in Champaran, Bihar. It was a civil disobedience movement where the people refused to do what the British rulers dictated. It was clear that indigo cultivation was not a problem in itself, but exploitation of workers and monoculture (growing only one crop) was bad for the ecology, and for the people. It was the first of many such movements that led to our country's freedom.

Chemical indigo dye was invented in Germany in 1878. But the demand for Indian plant-based 'blue gold' continues. People believe it has curative properties. In towns like Kongarapattu in Tamil Nadu, the highest indigo-producing state, newborn babies are swaddled in the cloth in which indigo leaves are filtered!

Jute Cultivation

Think about the tonnes of things that have been moved from one part of the world to another – sugar, mangoes, spices, potatoes, onions – how could they have been packed if there were no gunny bags? Jute was the second most-used natural fibre in the world after cotton till the mid-twentieth century. And the top producer of jute was undivided India.

Jute is a fibre obtained from the stems of several plant species of the Corchorus family, with *Corchorus olitorius* (tossa jute) and *Corchorus capsularis* (white jute) most commonly grown in India. That the fibre was used as ropes or as cloth in the pottery making process has been found in IVC sites.

Historians believe jute was introduced to Indus Valley sometime before 2000 BCE. In undivided Bengal, the jute plant has been used for thousands of years, both for its edible leaves and for the fibre that could be spun into cloth or ropes. When the Dutch East India Company discovered the strength and versatility of the fibre, they took back shiploads of the fibre to Europe. Next, the British transported it from Bengal to England. They also discovered that a jute bag filled with sand was the easiest and most economical way of stopping a bullet. So now, jute became important not just for cloth, and rope for ships, but also for the military. The British rulers in India were quick to set up jute mills and get Indian farmers to go all out to produce jute. Millions of bags of sandbags were exported from Bengal during World War I. India remains the top producer of jute in the world. Now that the world knows the ill-effects of plastic packaging, there is a renewed interest in jute packaging. With new technology and vastly improved agricultural practices, jute production is set to rise again. Apart from traditional usage, the 'golden fibre' is also being used to make car panels, sneakers and soft, breathable fabric, including sarees!

JACKFRUIT

What's cauliflory? No, no, not wrongly spelt cauliflower. It is the botanical term to describe a fruit that grows directly from the trunk and lower branches of a tree, like the jackfruit. The largest tree-borne fruit in the world, the jackfruit (*Artocarpus heterophyllus*) originated in the Western Ghats, the biodiversity-rich mountain range along India's southwestern border. It is native to Malaysia and Borneo too, and researchers believe jackfruits were domesticated and cultivated simultaneously and independently both in India and in Southeast Asia for thousands of years.

It is a miracle of nature that the fruit has such thick, spiky skin and a sticky fibrous layer to cushion the sweet lumps of fruit called achenes, each containing one waxy oblong seed. The fleshy pods, when unripe, are cooked to make curries and as a substitute for meat because of their texture. When ripe, they are fragrant and sweet and eaten as a fruit. In Kerala, jackfruit can be included in the starters, main course, dessert or as a snack at any time of the day. It is a good source of energy, protein, minerals and vitamins. Some people eat it with honey. The seeds too can be cooked or roasted like groundnuts and chestnuts and eaten as a snack or added to sambars and gravies. The leaves are used as fodder and in lieu of parchment paper to steam special dishes. The tree is also cultivated for its timber, since it is resistant to termites and fungus. The dye from the trunk is used to colour the robes worn by Buddhist monks in some countries.

So, does this spiky tree get its name because it is the jack of all trades? No, that credit goes to the Malayalam word *chakka* which itself may have come from *che-kai*, meaning 'bunch of green unripe fruit'. When the 16th-century Portuguese physician and herbalist Garcia da Orta saw the fruit during his explorations, he noted it down as 'jaca'. It became jackfruit in English. But for how long have humans known about it? Its Sanskrit name *panasa* may be of indigenous Munda origin, and finds mention in the Ramayana, and in the *Brihat Samhita* written in the 6th century CE. This text also gives instructions on how the tree can be grafted and maintained. Even earlier, the jackfruit, or *pala* in Tamil finds several mentions in Tamil Sangam poems, composed roughly between 300 BCE and 300 CE.

The first foreigner to have mentioned this fruit during the 7th century was Xuanzang, also called Hiuen Tsang. Moroccan traveller Ibn Battuta (1304 CE–1377 CE) described the jackfruit as having the 'rind of an ox' in his book *The Travels of Ibn Battuta*. He also mentioned the two types of the fruit, *barki* which grew near the ground, and *shaki* that grew higher up, as the best of all fruits of Hindustan.

Archaeological sites in Narhan in present-day Uttar Pradesh revealed the remains of jackfruit, believed to be from 1100 BCE to 800 BCE. Wood charcoal remains of jackfruit were also discovered in the archaeological site in Senuwar (now Bihar). These were not forest areas. This led scientists to believe that ancient humans may have procured seeds from southern India to create forests in north India. The tropical fruit moved through trade to different parts of the world including the Americas. In Sri Lanka, it is said that 'with a jak and a coconut in your backyard you will never starve'. In fact, in 1915, philanthropist Arthur V. Dias imported jackfruit seedlings from Malaysia with the aim to plant one million of them in Sri Lanka. This movement to ensure food security became so popular that he earned the name Kos Mama, or Jackfruit Uncle.

Jackfruit is the national fruit of Sri Lanka and Bangladesh. In India, jackfruit is the state fruit of Kerala and Tamil Nadu. Panruti is known as the 'Jackfruit capital of India', and its fruits have a GI tag. India is the largest producer of jackfruit in the world. Apart from its many traditional uses, unripe jackfruit is also fast becoming a meat substitute among vegans.

From Tree to Pillar

Have you been to the 16th-century Padmanabhapuram Palace? You'll find many beautifully carved pillars in this UNESCO World Heritage site. One particular pillar called *kannithoonu* is carved out of a single massive trunk of a jackfruit tree.

JATAKA TALES

We all know what happened to the tortoise that couldn't keep quiet when it was being transported through the air by two geese. In the *Katha Sarita Sagara*, written by Somadeva Bhatta in Sanskrit, somewhere around 1070 CE in Kashmir, the name of the tortoise is Kambugriva, and the two swans are Vikata and Sankata. In the Jataka (meaning 'birth stories') version, the tale is a story inside a story. Two wild ducks befriend the tortoise, and they agree to carry him to the Himalayas. On the way, the tortoise hears people on the ground talking. He wants to reply to them, opens his mouth and... thud! He lands in the open courtyard in the palace of Brahmadatta, the king of Benares. The notoriously talkative king wonders how a tortoise could have landed from the sky. His wise adviser says it is the plight of all who talk more than necessary. In the Jataka Tales, the adviser is a Bodhisattva, the Buddha in an earlier life.

The Buddha had many followers. When he died around 483 BCE, they decided to write down his teachings and put them in three sections called *tripitakas*, literally meaning 'three baskets'. One of the baskets contained stories that came to be called the Jataka. The Jataka are moral stories about Bodhisattva, often taking the form of animals, humans and other creatures. It is believed that the Buddha could recall anecdotes from his previous births, and that he used these to illustrate his messages in the present. This gave rise to the tale-within-a-tale, three-tier format. One part is set in the present, the second is a story from a previous birth and the third is the link between the two.

But what or who is a Bodhisattva? One sect of Buddhists called Theravada, believe that Siddhartha Gautama took many forms, each called a Bodhisattva, in his previous births on his way to becoming the Enlightened One, the Buddha. Believers of Mahayana Buddhism believe that there are many Buddhas, and that all Bodhisattvas aim to become enlightened like the Buddha.

By most accounts, there are 547 Jataka tales collected between the 3rd century BCE and the 2nd century CE. The stories bring out morals that are applicable to people of all ages. Contrary to popular belief, the tales are not strictly for children, as they are more about traders, travels and ethical practices. The stories bring out the four common reasons for evil actions – dislike, partiality, ignorance and fear.

If you've been to Sanchi, you may have seen a railing depicting the Mahakapi Jataka, a story about the Bodhisattva as a king of monkeys. The sculpture, possibly from circa 1st century CE, shows the monkey king stretching his body across the Ganga so that the other monkeys could use it as a bridge and escape to safety. This is an early archaeological evidence of the Jataka Tales. The tales travelled to different lands through people who travelled on the silk routes and on the marine routes.

If you meet a stranger during your vacation in a new land, or a tourist in your homeland, you may strike up a conversation about the transport, or a sports event or a new app, maybe. (What would you talk about?) Traders on ancient routes discussed culture and philosophy and traded stories like the Jataka. Some of the tales mention Suvarnadvipa (parts of present-day Southeast Asia), Ratnadvipa (present-day Sri Lanka), and Baveru (ancient Babylonia).

As Buddhism spread, so did the tales. Or, it could be that as the Jataka spread, so did the rise of Buddhism. The universal messages of righteous action helped each region to adapt the stories, many of which share the same plots as the Panchatantra and Aesop's Fables. In the modern world, the Jataka Tales have been presented as plays, and other forms of visual and performing arts.

Parrot Puzzles

How many tales do you know that feature parrots? Here are some glimpses of tales from the Jataka.

Two parrot brothers are separated at birth. One is raised by thieves and the other is raised by sages. What do you think happens to the brothers in the story?

The Bodhisattva, as a parrot king, is very loyal to a fig tree even when it grows very old. Moved by the parrot's loyalty, Sakka, the king of gods, restores the tree.

There's also one where a parrot is trained to spy for a king.

KABADDI

Would you like to test your lung power? Take a deep breath, and then start chanting 'kabaddi, kabaddi, kabaddi, kabaddi...' as you breathe out. See how long you can go before taking another gulp of air. Twenty times? More? Now, try repeating this feat while running, crouching or trying to catch a slippery friend or sibling. It requires lung power, physical strength, focus, swiftness and skill. Kabaddi is a game that requires all of these.

The Mahabharata tells us, Krishna played this game in Vrindavan. The *chakravyuha* episode in the Kurukshetra war is believed to have used moves similar to that in kabaddi, where a soldier goes into an offensive circle. According to Buddhist writings, young Siddhartha, who would become the Buddha, also played kabaddi with his friends in Nepal. It is known by different names in different parts of India – *hu-tu-tu* in the west and north, *ha-do-do* in the east (and in Bangladesh) and *chedugudu* in the south.

The game may also have been inspired by Tamil Nadu's *jallikattu* where players aim to catch a bull by its horns. In fact, the game may have got its name from the Tamil term *kai* (hand) *pidi* (hold/catch), though in Tamil, the game is called *sadugudu* more often than kabaddi. According to

Sangam literature, *sadugudu* has been played for at least 2,000 years. Similar to how a *jallikattu* player goes into the arena, trying to tame a bull without touching it, in kabaddi too, a player goes in to tame one or more opponents and bring them over, across the dividing line, to the home side. The difference is that in kabaddi, you have to touch an opponent. It used to be played in the gurukuls.

Kabaddi is played by two teams, each with seven players in most versions of the game. A 'raider' from team A moves to the opposite side and tries to 'catch' one or more opponents and drag them back across the line. Simultaneously, when the raider touches an opponent, team B tries to hold him back. It is a tough game of wrestling, tag, tug-of-war and breath control all at once.

The game spread to other Asian countries from the Indian subcontinent. Buddhist monks took it as far as Japan. Iranians believe they too have known an almost identical game called Zu, for about 2,000 years. Played just for fun with the chant of 'zouuuu, zouuuu', it gave way to the organized game of kabaddi after the formation of their kabaddi federation in 1996. In Sri Lanka, it is called *gudu* and in Thailand, it is *theechub*. The game was showcased at the 1936 Olympic Games in Berlin. While it did not catch on internationally then, it did stay as a popular game of the masses in Asia. It required no expense, could be played on any piece of land and was a great way to keep your body and mind fit and alert.

India first made formal rules for the game in 1923. The Kabaddi Federation of India was born in 1950. Since then, India has taken the game to many countries. According to the World Kabaddi Organization, more than 50 million people play this game in sixty-five countries including the

USA, Canada, Italy and Japan. Till 2025, India has been the winner in all the World Cup tournaments in the popular version, and Iran has been the runners-up! However, in other tournaments like the 2018 Asian Games, South Korea beat India in an early round.

KATHAK

Watching a good Kathak performance can be mesmerizing with the swift pirouettes, the rhythmic footwork (called *tatkaar*), the beautiful costumes and the vibrant music with the *ta thei tat* sounds. But Kathak is more than just this. It is a dance form that actually started as a storytelling practice by nomadic bards. It evolved by imbibing and sharing influences with other forms of dance. What we know as Kathak, one of the eight classical dance forms of India, is a beautiful fusion of many cultures.

Let's start at a known beginning. During Vedic times, Kathakas was the name given to wandering storytellers who told a story or 'katha'. The Kathakas conveyed the stories from the great Indian epics using a combination of poetry, music and dance. They were also fearless when it came to debate and discussion.

When invaders, starting with Alexander of Macedonia, came into northern India through the mountain passes of the northwest, they left behind some cultural influences. These can be seen in our dance forms, including the *nartan* (or dance) practised by the Kathakas. Dance researchers have found impressions of *ghungroos* (or ankle-bells) in a Grecian urn that is before the time of the *Natyashastra*.

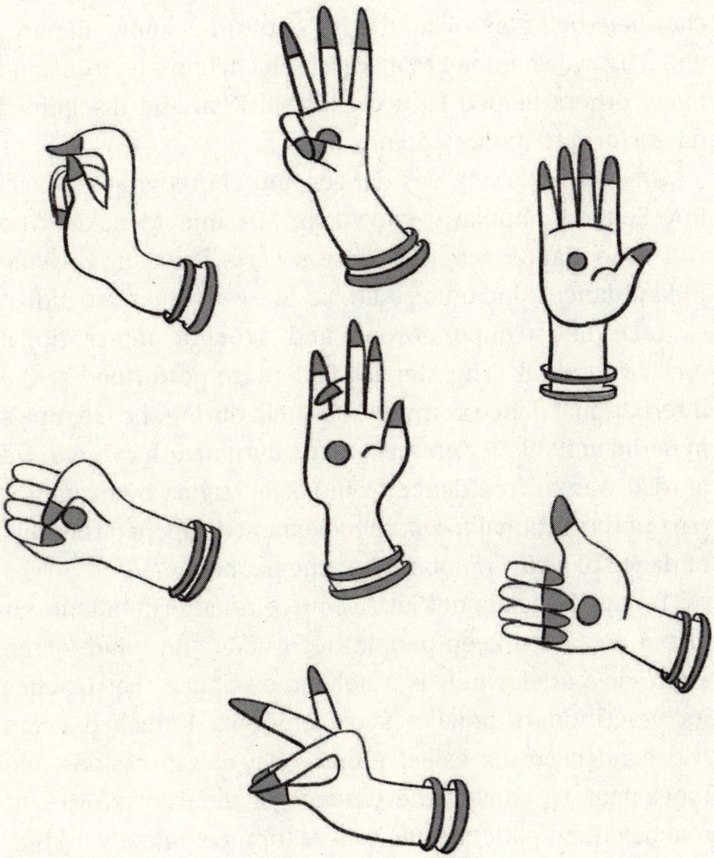

Some limb movements are similar to those in Greek theatre called Yavana. Some steps are similar to those in the flamenco dance.

Nartan flourished in the temples of the north during the Bhakti Movement of the 15th century. With time, the devotional storytelling entered Mughal courts. Costumes became more Persian. It was only in the early 1900s that the name 'Kathak' came to be used for the dance. Different styles, attributed to different *gharanas* evolved, the major *gharanas* being associated with Jaipur, Lucknow, Benares and Raigarh. Shambhu Maharaj of the Lucknow *gharana* and many others helped to take this spiritual and disciplined dance form to more people.

One such person was dancer and choreographer Leila Roy-Sokhey, popularly known as Madame Menaka, who started a dance school and was very active in reviving Indian dances, including Kathak. She was the first Indian to take her troupe abroad and brought international focus on Kathak. The Menaka Ballet also performed at the international dance competitions held during the Olympics in Berlin in 1936. Her greatest contribution both in India and abroad was to free dance from social stigma by making it part of the national freedom movement. It opened the field of dance to a vast number of young people.

Today, Kathak is not just a source of entertainment but also a means to keep people fit in body and mind. As an expressive art form, it is a holistic discipline that teaches its practitioners how to show emotion. Kathak dancers use hand gestures called mudras, facial expressions and movement to convey the essence of different stories. It teaches them patience and makes for a complete workout. No wonder it is an accredited course in many foreign universities too.

KHAKI

During the initial British rule of India, soldiers wore bright scarlet coats as part of their uniforms. Must look striking, of course, but can you imagine how the soldiers would stand out in the war zone? Indian soldiers recruited to the British forces also wore red. In the 19th century, the British were engaged in small wars in different parts of India. The scarlet uniforms were hardly any good as camouflage.

In 1846, the British East India Company formed the Corps of Guides, which regulated Indian soldiers who fought on behalf of the British Indian Army. Sir Harry Lumsden, founder of this body, declared that he would make the Guides 'invisible in a land of dust'. And how did he do it? Along with his second-in-command William Hodson, he came up with the idea of dust-coloured uniforms. At first, the uniforms were stitched with white cloth dyed in mud. Next, tea was used as a dye. Later, John Haller, a German textile engineer and missionary working at the Basel Mission Weaving Establishment in Balmatta, Mangalore, invented the khaki dye using oil extracted from cashew shells. By 1852, khaki material began to be produced in Mangalore. It became the material for police uniforms in the Canara district. When Lord Roberts, the British governor of the Madras

Presidency learnt about this material, he recommended its use in military uniforms.

Sir Herbert Benjamin, a soldier and official in the British Indian administration, was a linguist, passing examinations in Urdu, Hindi and Persian. According to the Oxford English Dictionary the first evidence of the use of the word khaki for the army uniform was by this person in a letter he wrote in 1857. *Khak* means dust in Urdu and Hindustani, and khaki means dust-coloured. The British started using khaki uniforms for their soldiers in India after the mutiny in 1857. (What did the mutiny have to do with uniforms? Check it out in *Travelling Treasures: 100 Incredible Tales of How Things Came to India.*) By 1897, British armies all over the world started using khakis. So visible – pun intended – was the benefit of having khaki uniforms, that many other countries too changed to khakis, including the United States of America.

Gradually, khaki – both the colour, and the material – became associated with people who worked outdoors. The uniforms of the police turned khaki. In the early 20th century, the cloth that was inspired by the dust and soil of India came to be used by fashion houses, especially in the US, to make trousers and shirts for adventure lovers, and from there for people who played polo and other outdoor sports.

In 1947, after India's Partition, the khakis gave way to olive green. While the Indian Army has different uniforms for different regions and purposes, the most common uniform is made with DCM – would you like to guess what that could mean? Digital Camouflage Material. If you were to get a chance to design your school uniform, which colour would it be? And why?

KHICHDI

When your body needs comfort, it's time to feed it some khichdi. Not the kind made in Emperor Akbar's royal kitchen with equal amounts of rice, lentils and ghee but the one prescribed by Ayurveda, with rice, lentils and just a dash of ghee and spices. We're talking about that melt-in-the-mouth, ghee-topped, warm food that you can spoon into your mouth on a cold day, or when you have a cold or are unwell. It is easy on the palate, easy on the stomach and totally healthy. Chanakya, the author of *Arthashastra* (yes, the same person mentioned on page xiii), suggested a very precise recipe: 1 prastha rice, 1/4 prastha lentil, 1/62 prastha salt and 1/6 prastha ghee. Cook it to a mush with water (oh no, he forgot to mention how many prastha of that!). Called *khicca* in Sanskrit, it has been eaten in India at least from the time Ayurveda has been practised. That's at least for 3,000 years now.

Many travellers to India have been smitten by the humble khichdi. Moroccan traveller Ibn Battuta wrote in the 14th century that in India people ate *kishri*. The basic dish involves dry roasting moong dal, and cooking it with rice, with just a bit of cumin and black pepper. Each part of the country and each family has its own variation to this mix, adding different things to the pot. Bengal has its bhoger khichuri, rich with seasonal vegetables. Tamil Nadu has its pongal, which is also the ceremonial dish made with newly harvested rice and lentils for the festival of Pongal. Both savoury and sweet pongals are made.

One of the earliest Europeans to travel to India after Italy's Niccolò de' Conti, was the Russian Afanasy Nikitin. He visited India around 1470 and wrote in his book *A Journey Beyond the Three Seas* (can you name these three seas?) how precious horses were in India, and how they were fed khichdi, made with sugar and ghee. Francisco Pelsaert, a Dutch businessman, made detailed notes about the food of India when he lived in Agra between 1620 and 1627. He too wrote in great detail about India's trade, rulers, religions and way of life in his book *Remonstrantie* (published as *Jahangir's India in English*). In the chapter 'The Manner of Life', he wrote about the monotonous food that the common people ate, sometimes 'nothing but a little "khichri" made of "green pulse" mixed with rice'. The ruler of Agra at that time, Jahangir, is believed to have elevated that common dish to something rich called lazeezan – by adding dry fruits and more spices.

The British recognized the goodness of khichdi and tried a variation. Back in England, they substituted the lentils with boiled eggs and a fish of their region, haddock. Voilà, the khichdi was now the porridge called *kedgeree*.

Indian khichdi is a dish that is now available all over the world. The Ayurvedic *khicca* may have had just three main ingredients, but an Indian restaurant in Dubai has become popular for serving a khichdi made with twenty ingredients procured from twenty different states and served on an India-shaped plate.

LEMON AND LIME

If you can tell the difference between lime and lemon, take a bow. In India, the two words are used interchangeably by most of us. What we know and what is important to us is that they're both sour, both can be squeezed to make juice, and both smell good! Technically though, lemons are bigger and more oval in shape with thicker skin than the smaller, rounder, thinner-skinned lime. All the lemons we use in the world now are hybrids, their ancient ancestors being the ancient citron.

The origins of lemons and limes are disputed. The most common assumption until recently has been that it could have originated in Southeast Asia, in the region extending from the foothills of northeastern Himalayas, eastward through the Malay Archipelago to China and Japan, and southward to Australia and also to New Caledonia and New Guinea. There are so many different kinds of lemons and limes that it is difficult to tell which one is the 'original'. Oranges, lemons, citron, grapefruit, pomelo and many other fruits are all called citrus fruits. They all have a common citrus-like ancestor. And where was this ancestor?

A genetic study published in *Nature Genetics* in 2023 makes a surprising revelation. The study believes that citrus-related fruits may have originated on the ancient Indian Plate moving towards Eurasia – millions of years before the formation of the Himalayas! Can you believe it?

The first citrus genus may have originated in the South China region based on the fact that citrus-like fossils were discovered there. Citrus like mandarins may have appeared in China eight million years ago. Other citrus species like pomelo and citron may have appeared in the Himalayan foothills of northeast India after this. All the citrus fruits that we enjoy today have been derived from three ancient ancestors – the citron (*Citrus medica*), the pomelo (*Citrus maxima*) and the mandarin (*Citrus reticulata*). With repeated and continuous cultivation, newer types have evolved.

Lemons were known in ancient India, say researchers, based on a lemon leaf-shaped pendant that date back to circa 3000 BCE. Made of steatite, a kind of rock, it was discovered in a Harappa site. By the 5th century BCE, citron had reached Persia. In 310 BCE, Greek philosopher Theophrastus first described the citron in his book *Historia Plantarum*, or *Enquiry into Plants*. During that time, the sour fruit was called 'median' or 'Persian apple'. By the first century CE, citrons and early lemons had reached Rome. They were considered exotic fruit and were flaunted by the rich.

Nearly a thousand years after that, in the 10th century, Arab traders took the fruits to new places. They called it *laymun*, and it is from here that the fruits came to be called lemons. Spanish and Portuguese explorers took them to the Americas too. During the bubonic plague in 1668, many Europeans were dying, except in the city of Paris. The reason? Lemon juice, which the Parisians had taken a liking to. Actually, the peels did it. They were thrown all over. As rats in gutters nibbled on the peels, they were taking in limonene, a chemical which killed the fleas and eggs that caused the plague.

The health benefits of lemons and lime and their ability to prevent scurvy lie in their rich reserves of vitamin C. India has many special regional citrus fruits, and many have Geographical Indication tags like the Kachai Champra of Manipur, Indi lime of Karnataka and Puliyankudi lime of Tamil Nadu. Time to go make yourself a glass of nimbu juice!

Art of the Arab Chests

When merchants from different lands left India, what did they take their merchandise in? Remember, no plastic bags or plywood crates then! Arab traders, who came from a largely treeless land, were fascinated by the beautiful teakwood chests made by Indian carpenters. Teakwood was available mostly in the Western Ghats in the south, and traded in the port of Calicut and in the Dangs and Panchmahals Forests of Gujarat.

Also made of shisham and rosewood, these large trunks were embellished with brass fittings. The Arabs carried these trunks from the western ports of India. When the Portuguese traders came to India, they brought their own chests which had 'feet' or fretted stands to elevate the trunk from the floor.

Indian carpenters liked this idea and started fitting these chests with stands too. From the Dutch invaders and their camphorwood chests, the carpenters learnt to add brass knobs and a back-plate. The idea to have three-ring padlocks came from Chinese chests. These chests also had internal cash-boxes, an idea probably borrowed from English chests. Over time, the Arab traders started using them not just as trunks during travel but also as prized furniture. The chests too were traded in different parts of the world, like East Africa. The Arabs also started making their own chests. Called Arab chests, these international chests with their humble beginnings in India are in high demand among antique collectors for their beauty and craftsmanship, and for the stories behind them.

LUDO

In 2024, a groom was caught on video playing ludo on his phone even while the wedding ceremony was going on! A friend posted the video, and it went viral. Whether it was the popularity of an online game, or the game of Ludo that interested netizens we do not know, but we're sure the inattentive groom must have got quite an earful from his new family.

Ludo, the popular board game, emerged from an ancient Indian game called Pachisi. The game consisted of a plus-shaped cloth marked with squares. Each arm had three rows, and the centre was called chowki. Players used five cowrie shells and moved their pawns forward based on the number they got. The maximum a throw could get was 25 or *pachees*, in Hindi and Urdu, and hence the name. The game has been played at least since the 6th century CE.

There were many games played with dice, and not all of them were called Pachisi. For long, people played the game by drawing the outline on the floor, the ground or on a flat stone. It was an easy game and easily brought families and friends together. Kings and queens loved it. Emperor Akbar is supposed to have loved the game too. He had a large outdoor Pachisi board built in one of the courtyards

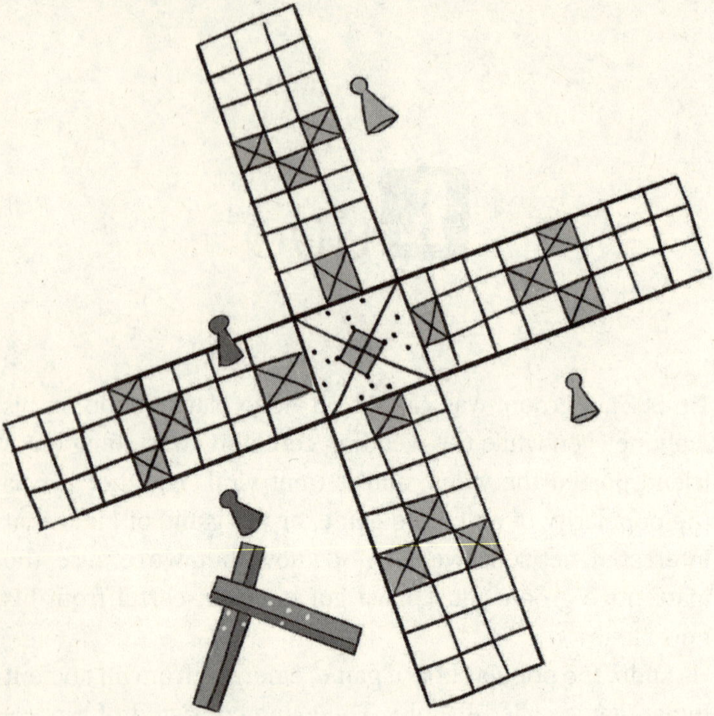

of Fatehpur Sikri. While the Pachisi court still exists, there is no proof of the legend that he played the game using women as the live game pieces. However, many writers of later times did write about his passion for the game. French traveller and photographer Louis Rousselet wrote about 'the game of pucheesee' and how women dressed in the players' colours moved on the floor in his 1876 book *India and Its Native Princes*.

When the British saw the game, they modified it. They laid out the cross on a square board and used dice instead of cowrie shells. In 1891, Alfred Collier patented the game and called it ludo, a word derived from the Latin phrase for

'I play'. He claimed that he was the inventor, even though it was a remake of Pachisi.

The English ludo became very popular, and each country had its own variation – the British Navy's Uckers, Sweden's Fia, Swiss Eile Mit weile, Spanish Parchis, Colombian Parqués, Vietnamese Cờ cá ngựa to name a few. The Pakistani ludo allowed players the choice of moving their pawns backward or forward. All the versions had one thing in common – they brought much fun and laughter into the room.

Bored? Get a Board Out!

Ludo regained much of its charm along with other board games during the pandemic of 2019. Pachisi is still played in many places in India. Have you played it yet? Visitors may find beautifully embroidered or coloured Pachisi boards that showcase India's history in the collections at the National Museum, New Delhi, the Swiss Museum of Games, the Children's Museum of Indianapolis, the Nasser D. Khalili Collection of Islamic Art (a moving collection) and in the Victoria and Albert Museum, London.

MADRAS CHECKS

If you wear a checked, or chequered shirt as part of your uniform, you may not think of it as something special. After all, you have to wear it every day. Ho-hum. What if the checks changed colour every time your shirt was washed? Would that be fun? Is that even possible?

Weavers in the village of Madrasapattinam, present-day metropolis Chennai, had for centuries been making pure cotton cloth with a combination of yarns dyed in at least two different colours. They used oil, indigo, rice gruel and turmeric to make the dyes. The result was a colourful smooth fabric with irregular checks. Fishermen and all the men of the area wore this and, like you, may not have thought much about the checks. In August 1639, two officials of the East India Company bought a piece of sandy beach from the Vijayanagar nayaka Damarla Venkatadri to set up the company's warehouse there. That's when Francis Day, one of the officials, noticed the checked fabric. He saw great potential for business and soon encouraged the weavers to produce more cloth that could be exported. As an incentive to the weavers, he proclaimed that they would not have to pay taxes for 30 years! Many weavers settled down in what the British called Madras. The cloth was sent to London and to places like Bantam in Indonesia and Manila in Philippines.

The East India exporters wanted to avoid paying tax. In those days, smaller lengths of cloth did not attract tax. In 1660, the wily merchants packaged the fabric in 8-metre-long pieces that could be cut to make three large square kerchiefs or scarves. They were called Madras Hand Kerchief. In the 19th century, a prefix was added and Real Madras Hand Kerchief became the specific trade name for the export quality fabric. 'Madras Checks' was the broad term for the pattern. It was traded with West Africa where people wore it as head covering, or for children's bedding. Portuguese traders bartered the cloth in England in exchange for slaves to be sent to the Portuguese colonies in the Americas.

In the 19th century, when slavery was abolished in the Caribbean, workers were brought from Madras in place of the now-free slaves who liked to wear the colourful Madras checks brought by them. The trend for colourful checks continues in these parts of the world.

According to a popular legend, Elihu Yale, who was appointed as president of Madras in 1687, donated books, money and bales of Madras checks to a college. It was such a big donation that it became possible to name a university after him! Two hundred years later, a company sold shirts made of Madras checks. Like always, the colours ran. The consumers were angry and threatened to take the manufacturers to court. The quick-thinking British advertisement genius, David Ogilvy, suggested the range be marketed with the tagline 'Guaranteed to Bleed'. The flaw became a selling point, and 'bleeding Madras', which changed colour after every wash became a huge success.

When students from the premier colleges including Yale on the east coast of USA went to play rugby, volleyball, swim and sunbathe in places like Bermuda in the Caribbean, they picked up Bermuda shorts made of Madras checks. This fabric has really had a chequered journey, right?

A City Called Chennaipattinam

Knowing a city's history is interesting. How did Chennai, capital of Tamil Nadu, get its name? The debate is still on. The name of the local ruler of the area long before East India Company arrived was Mutharasa. *Pattinam* in Tamil means city. Could the place have therefore been called Mutharasapattinam, which flowed out of the mouth as Madrasapattinam? Or from the Church of Madre de Deus built by the Portuguese in the area? Or after the wealthy Portuguese family called Madeiros who lived there? When the British bought the place from Damarla Venkatadri Nayakudu, he called it Chennaipattinam after his father Damarla Chennappa Nayakudu. Or, was it called that after the Chenna Kesava Perumal Temple? The British chose to call it Madras. In 1996, the city that became famous for its textiles and Madras checks, was officially renamed Chennai.

MANGO

This sweet fruit can cause many a family fights over things such as which variety is the sweetest, or which form – ice cream, *aamras*, milkshake – is the best! But everyone agrees that mango is one of the most popular fruits in the world.

Mango, scientifically named *Mangifera indica L.* has its origin in the foothills of the Himalayas in the Indo-Burma-Malay region. It has been cultivated in India for 5,000 to 6,000 years. The Mahabharata and Buddhist texts have several mentions of the fruit. Mangoes have been found inscribed on gateways to the stupas in Bharhut and Sanchi dating back to 110 CE. (A mango tree features in a Jataka tale too. More about Jataka tales on page 90.) Buddhist scholar Faxian in the 5th century CE mentioned that a mango orchard was gifted to Gautama Buddha as a place to rest. Xuanzang in the 7th century is believed to be the first to have introduced it to people outside India. Other people like 10th-century Arab geographer Ibn-Hawqal were also fascinated by the fruit.

Mango became known to China and Southeast Asia in the 7th century, East Africa in the 10th century and to the Philippines in the 15th century, through Spanish travellers.

Every part of India had its own variety of mango, and the people were happy sucking on the juicy fruit. Then came the

Portuguese. Much as they liked the taste, they did not like that it had so much fibre, and that it could not always be cut neatly into pieces to be eaten at their tables. The Jesuit priests in the Konkan region of Goa got into the act of trying to graft different varieties and finally hit upon a delicious, smooth variety. The fruit was named Alphonso after the Portuguese viceroy Afonso (yes, right, easier to spell than the pricey fruit variety) de Albuquerque, who had a big part in laying the foundations for the Portuguese rule in India. Called *hapus* in Maharashtra and *hafus* in Gujarat, alphonso mangoes now grow best in areas such as Ratnagiri.

Akbar, meanwhile, who did not like the Portuguese much, tolerated them because they had come up with many varieties of mangoes. He even had an orchard in Darbhanga planted with 1,00,000 mango saplings. His grandson Shah Jahan was equally fond of the fruit, and had a special route marked between Konkan and Delhi so he could get the fastest delivery of fresh mangoes!

The seeds of the fruit were carried by travellers and traders to different parts of the world and cultivation began in all the tropical regions like Brazil, Mexico, Egypt and Israel. It was also grown in Florida. Now, many orchards in the world have mangoes grown from Florida seeds.

India retains its position as the world's largest producer of mangoes.

Incredible Mangoes

• Mangoes and poison ivy are botanically related – they both belong to the family *Anacardiaceae*. Not just that, their other relatives are cashew and pistachios. All of them contain a compound called urushiol, which is the one that is an irritant. But thankfully, this exists only in the white sap, not in the fruit.

• Mango is the national fruit of India, Pakistan and Philippines.

• Amrapali, Banganapalli, Badami, Chausa, Safeda, Dasheri, Kesar, Himsagar, Langra, Malgova, Sadabahar, Rajapuri and Jardalu are some famous varieties of mangoes. What are the most loved mangoes in your state?

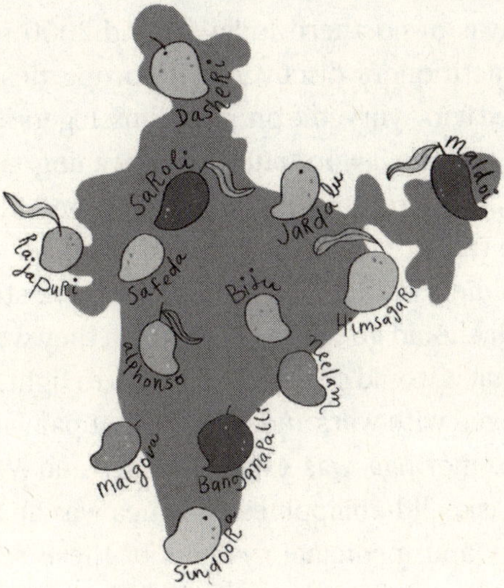

Moringa

We call this vegetable drumsticks. What moringa needs is a loud drumroll for being not just a super nutritious vegetable but also for being an easy to grow, hardy tree capable of addressing the problems of climate change.

Moringa oleifera is a native of India, Pakistan and Nepal. It is believed to have been first discovered in the foothills of the Himalayas in northern India around 2000 BCE. Ancient medical practitioners discovered its properties very early and included it in Ayurvedic preparations. It gets its scientific name from the Tamil word *murungai* meaning 'twisted pod'. Every part of the tree has many uses. The long, slender seed pods of the tree are what are called drumsticks.

If the soldiers of the Mauryan Empire were strong, some of the credit should go to moringa, which they were given in the belief that it would give them stamina to fight, relieve the stress involved with wars and help to treat pain and injuries. With trade, moringa was taken to East and West Africa, Southeast Asia and Philippines. Moringa was absorbed into the culinary and medicinal systems of these regions. The Greeks discovered the many benefits of moringa and even used its oil as sunscreen. The benefits of moringa then became known to the Roman Empire. The Egyptians also used moringa oil – jars of moringa oil have been found in ancient Egyptian tombs.

In modern times, the tree has an important role in climate management. When drought hit Tunisia, a project called Acacias for All was started. Led by a French–Tunisian activist, rural women planted over 50,000 moringa plants. With their deep roots capable of drawing out water, the trees flourished causing the area to beat drought. The forest of moringa trees served as good protection against sand and wind blowing in the region. With all its wonderful properties, the moringa tree ought to be grown in every house. It can also be grown in a pot. The downside? Bark-eating caterpillars and hairy caterpillars love the tree too, and don't like it if you come close to them.

The Miracle Tree

- While oranges are tastier, moringa seed and leaf extracts contain seven times more vitamin C than oranges, 17 times more calcium than milk, ten times more vitamin A than carrots, nine times more protein than yogurt, 15 times more potassium than banana and 25 times more iron than spinach. Should you therefore have drumsticks by the kilogram? No! It just means you should consume it in some form regularly along with a variety of other foods.
- India is the largest producer of moringa in the world. It grows well all over India and is cultivated extensively in Tamil Nadu and Kerala.

MULLIGATAWNY SOUP

What does Charles Dickens have to do with a spicy hot soup born in India? He owned and edited a magazine called *All the Year Round* in which his own story *A Tale of Two Cities* was serialized. The August 1868 issue of the magazine carried a recipe for mulligatawny soup. 'Take two quarts of water, my lord, and boil a fowl; then add to it a whole white onion...'

Mulligatawny soup gets its name from the humble *milagu thanneer*, Tamil for pepper water. In South India, rasam is an everyday dish, made by boiling tamarind and other ingredients in *thanneer*, also called *thanni*. One of them is the basic pepper rasam made with tamarind, tomatoes, salt and pepper, and garnished with mustard, asafoetida and curry leaves. Best served hot with freshly made rice and a dollop of ghee, this is comfort food that is good for the digestive system and for the days when you have cold, cough or a sore throat.

The British used this hot soup as a digestive before or after a meal. But since the local way of having it was too fiery for their palate, they adapted it with additions of their own. They added 'onions browned gently in some butter'. Soon, other things went into the pot; one recipe suggested 'young rabbit' while others recommended adding ham, beef, bacon or specific parts like a head, a knee or heel. The first recorded mention of the word 'mulligatawny' was in 1784, according to *Hobson-Jobson: A Glossary of Colloquial Anglo-Indian Words and Phrases.*

One of the earliest recipes may have been that of Scottish woman Stephana Malcolm. Her beautifully hand-written book of 1791 is still preserved in a digital archive of the National Library of Scotland. She learnt the intricacies of Indian recipes from her brothers who worked for the East India Company in India. When the members of the East India Company went back to England from Madras, they spread the word about this easy and nourishing soup. By the 1850s, mulligatawny sauce was available in tins, and the merchants carried them all the way to Africa. After some years, mulligatawny was also available as soup mix.

Mulligatawny was so popular in the Madras Presidency that a Britisher who served there earned the nickname Mull. (By the way, a Britisher serving in Bengal was called Qui-hi from the Hindustani phrase '*koi hai?*', and his contemporary in Bombay [now Mumbai] was called a Duck, after the fish Bombay Duck.) The humble *milagu thanni* went through many alterations and was even served in high and mighty dinners as 'Potage de Madras' or 'Consommé à l'indienne'. It made it to many parts of the world including popular TV shows in America.

What's in a Name?

Why would a fish be called a duck? Bombil, scientifically known as *Harpadon nehereus*, is a popular fish that is available in Bombay and the Konkan Coast. The colonial Britishers loved this fish. It was dried and transported all the way by mail trains to Calcutta. Mail is called *daak* in Bengali and many Indian languages. The Britishers heard it as duck. And soon, the fish that came by train became famous as Bombay Duck.

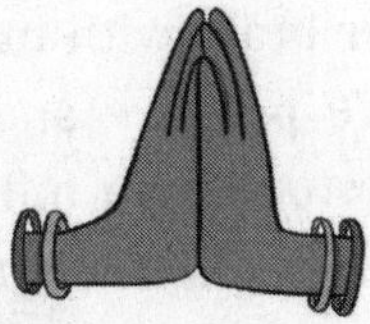

NAMASTE

Namaste, dear reader! A namaste is more than just a greeting. When said with intent, it could be used to convey welcome, thank you, respect, a fond farewell or more. It is a gesture immediately recognized by people all over the world as Indian, even though it is used in many Asian countries.

Where and when did namaste first come into use? No one knows, but it has been around for ages. The phrase is used in the Rig Veda which is believed to have been compiled somewhere in the 2nd millennium (that's over 3,500 years ago). The word is derived from the Sanskrit words *namas* meaning 'bow' and *te* meaning 'you', to mean 'I bow to you.' It shows humility, not servility. It is a gesture that says, 'I respect you'. It is also a gesture of prayer. It doesn't matter who you pray to or where, the intentional act of putting your palms together in front of your heart and bowing just a little helps you concentrate on your prayer. A namaste with your eyes closed makes the mind a little calmer too. Would you like to try it now, before you move to the next paragraph?

The namaste gesture is called Anjali mudra in yoga and is usually done at the start and end of your yoga session. The mudra helps you to focus. (And if you can't focus, don't worry and crowd your brain with more thoughts – it just means you need more practice and patience.) Scientific research says that gestures can influence how we think. What do you think the act of doing a namaste may signal to your brain? Think about it...

While namaste – both the word and the gesture – became common practice in India, the gesture of greeting moved to the rest of the world too. Yoga was one of the vehicles that made the phrase travel out of India. As the practice of yoga spread, so did the greeting and the mudra. In Thailand, the gesture is *wai*, *sembah* in Indonesia and *sampeah* in Cambodia.

The word appeared in English newspapers in India in the 1920s. When India gained Independence, the world press wrote about how Jawaharlal Nehru, the country's first prime minister closed his palms in a namaste, and when Mahatma Gandhi died, the word was used in the world press again. For a word that became known to the world so many years ago, it came into the English dictionary only in the 1940s.

While all this happened much before you were born, do you know what made it popular in recent times? The COVID-19 pandemic. For hundreds of years Indians had believed that 'touching' caused germs to jump from one person to another. Hungarian physician Ignaz Semmelweis thought the same and insisted that surgeons wash their hands before operating upon a patient. But this early pioneer of antiseptic hand-washing was laughed at, and the poor man was later sadly sent to a mental asylum. However, during the pandemic, people all over the world stopped hugging and shaking hands and instead used a wise old way of greeting – Namaste!

NEEM

The neem tree used to be called the village dispensary. Stomach needs a clean-up? Just chew some tender leaves. Scrapped your knee? Crush some leaves and cover the wound with the juice. Locals would know how to use the leaves, flowers, seeds or bark to cure a problem. The first part of its scientific name *Azadirachta indica* A. *Juss* comes from the Persian words *azad* (free), *dirakt* (tree) and *e-Hind* (of Indian origin), meaning 'the free tree of India'. And why was it free? The name comes from the tree's ability to stay free of problems caused by pests and insects.

Neem has been used in Ayurveda, Unani and Siddha systems of healthcare for over 2,000 years. People in the IVC too used it as medicine. The seeds, leaf and bark are used to make fertilizers, cosmetics and insecticides. Neem's antiseptic properties make it much in demand to make medicines not just for humans but also for cattle and livestock. The best *kajal* was made with the lampblack collected from lighting a wick dipped in neem oil. Its Sanskrit name *nimba* means 'bestower of good health'. The other name, *ravisambha*, indicates that neem is 'like the sunrays' that provide good health.

Most studies believe it may have originated along the Siwalik Range of the Himalayas in Assam and the Indochina region including Burma. From here, it was introduced to the rest of the Indian subcontinent that includes Bangladesh, Ceylon, India, Maldives, Nepal and Pakistan. As early as the second century CE, people in Southeast Asia had begun using neem from India and even started brushing their teeth with neem twigs. Emigrants and traders took neem to places like Fiji, Mauritius and Guyana. Many texts including palm-leaf texts of the 16th century from Bali mention neem.

The Portuguese called the tree *amargosa*, meaning 'bitter'. The British, much later, made it *margosa*. Sometime after 1558, Portuguese botanist and physician, Garcia de Orta became the first European to describe many of India's native plants of medical importance. His book in 1563 was translated into English and was called *Colloquies on the Simples and Drugs of India*. Guess who benefited from the goodness of neem? His horses! 'Neem tree has great repute as valuable and medicinal. The sore backs of horses that were most difficult to clean and heal were very quickly cured with the neem leaves pounded, mixed with lime juice, putting over the sores,' he wrote.

In the 19th century, the British introduced neem to their colonies in Sudan, and East and West Africa. They considered the fast-growing, hardy, no-maintenance trees to be excellent as shade providers. Neem propagates naturally through seeds. While fruits are cleaned to get seeds, the cultivators in Togo and Senegal leave the chore to fruit bats and birds, who eat the sweet pulp and then spit out the seeds under the trees.

Even though neem's insect-repellent properties were well-known and used in the Indian subcontinent for hundreds of years, scientists started research on neem as an insect repellent only in the 1920s. Their research did not get much publicity. But, in 1959, a German entomologist saw how locusts in Sudan never attacked the neem trees. In 1961, his study as well as those of some Indian scientists was recognized and scientists all over the world became aware of this wonder tree.

A report published by the National Academy of Sciences, Washington, titled *Neem: A Tree for Solving Global Problems* calls it a fascinating tree that could benefit every person on this planet. It could be used to 'reduce erosion, deforestation, and the excessive temperature of an overheated globe'.

Time to plant a neem sapling in your school! And eat up the *bevu-bella* (Kannada for neem-jaggery) mix offered during festivals such as Ugadi and Gudi Padwa. And do try neem preparations like *vepampoo rasam* made in Tamil Nadu and *neem begun* in Bengal.

Shade for Pilgrims

In the 1980s, over 50,000 neem saplings were planted in the hot plains of Arafat, to provide shade to the millions of pilgrims who come to Makkah. Desalted seawater was used to grow neem along avenues and parks in Qatar and Abu Dhabi. The Yunnan province in China has over 4,00,000 neem trees making it one of the largest neem plantations.

ORANGE

Ah, the fresh smell of a sweet orange! In Tamil, *narumanam* means fragrance, and from its root word *naru* comes the Sanskrit word *naranga*. The orange is called *narangi* in Hindi, *narandj* in Arabic, *narang* in Persian, *naranza* in Venetian Europe and *arancia* (with the initial 'n' dropped) in Italian. But where did the orange originate?

Like all citrus fruits, the orange too owes its lineage to the ancient citrus-like genus which may have ridden on the Indian Plate millions of years ago. (Have you read about Lime yet? On page 103.) The last common ancestor of all the citruses close to an orange (as different from lemon and lime) is believed to have originated some eight million years ago in the region that includes the foothills of the Himalayas, northeast India, northern Myanmar and the Yunnan province of southwest China. While the origin of orange is still disputed, most botanical research believes in this origin.

Japanese botanist Chōzaburō Tanaka was one of the earliest scientists to declare the Indian origin of oranges in 1928. During the course of his work, he also came up with 180 botanical names for different types of citrus fruits including the *Citrus indica* Tanaka. Called the Indian wild orange (though it is also believed to be a hybrid), it was discovered deep in the Garo Hills of Meghalaya in 1984. This ancient species is considered by many to be the parent – scientists use the word progenitor – of all citrus fruits. The region is in the Nokrek Biosphere, a part of which has been designated as the National Citrus Gene Sanctuary.

The sour or bitter orange was a hybrid that happened either in southern China or northern Indochina. It was introduced to Oman and later to Mesopotamia (most of modern-day Iraq along with parts of Syria, Türkiye and Iran) and from there to the eastern Mediterranean regions only in the 10th century. In Europe, it was written about as a plant with beautifully coloured fruits and was grown more as a decorative plant than for its edible fruit.

In his book, *Thirty Years in India* published in 1839, Major H. Bevan wrote about the orange thus, 'The greatest ornament of the gardens is a description of orange-tree, called cintra or coolang.' He later adds that people believe the fruit was brought to the region by the Portuguese, '...Some, however, believe that the great superiority of the coolang orange is owing to grafting and budding, a system in which the native gardeners at Nagpore are pre-eminently skilful.'

Today, oranges grow all over the world. But there may be a bit of India in many. For instance, the rare Tahiti orange is a descendent of the Indian Rangpur lime. The fruit that looks like an orange-coloured lime was introduced to the faraway island of Tahiti in the 1800s and tastes like pineapple, according to some people.

PANCHATANTRA

Long, long ago, there lived a monkey who was friends with a crocodile until... Oh, you know that story? Long, long ago there was a jackal who turned blue because... Oh, you know that too? Let's try another one then.

Long, long ago, thousands of years ago in a city called Mahilaropyam, in southern India, lived a king named Amarashakti. He thought that his three sons Bhaushakti, Ugrashakti and Anantashakti were very poor learners. One of his advisors, a man called Sumati, suggested that instead of teaching them the scriptures, sciences, politics and diplomacy, they should be told stories that brought out the wisdom in these disciplines. He also said that Visnusarman (or Vishnu Sarma), an expert in *nitishastra*, or the science of ethics, associated with Taxila, the world-famous university, would be just right for this work. So, the pundit was summoned, possibly from Kashmir, and the lessons began. Or rather, the storytelling began.

Panchatantra is the name given to the compilation of the eighty-seven stories that Visnusarman told the princes. He compiled the stories in five books: *Mitra-bheda* (The Loss of Friends), *Mitra-labha* (The Winning of Friends), *Kakolookiyam* (Of Crows and Owls), *Labdha-pranasam* (Loss of Gains) and *Apariksitakarakam* (Ill-Considered Actions). Panchatantra is definitely easier on the tongue than the other names it may have been known by – Tantrakhyayika, Panchakhyanaka or Tantropakhyana. We don't know how old the stories in the Panchatantra are, but we do know that Visnusarman – who too may be real or an imaginary literary character in the Panchatantra itself – is believed to have started compiling these stories somewhere between 3rd century BCE and 5th century CE. Almost everyone agrees that the stories are educative and entertaining.

Around 550 CE, Persian physician Borzuya was sent to India by the Sasanian king Khosrow I to find the plant that could revive the dead. Was it the sanjivini that is mentioned in the Ramayana? Did he find it? We don't know. A philosopher is believed to have told Borzuya that what he should be looking for was not a magic potion, but a book called the Panchatantra. Borzuya read the copy of it kept in a palace, memorized it during the day and secretly took notes at night, and once back in Persia, he translated it as *Kalilah wa Dimnah*. This is believed to be Panchatantra's first translation into a foreign language. Sadly, this Pahlavi version does not exist now, but a part of its Syrian translation called *Kalilag and Damanag* does.

The two jackals Karataka and Damanaka in the original Panchatantra became Kalilag and Damanag in Persia. In Arabic, they are called Kalila and Dimna, and their names changed when their story went to Germany, of course. The two jackals, one cunningly clever and another wisely noble, became Calila and Dimna when they were translated into old Castilian.

Panchatantra is believed to have inspired *The Arabian Nights* (originally called *Alf Laylah wa-Laylah* in Arabic, or *One Thousand and One Nights*). It was translated from Sanskrit into Pahlavi, Arabic, Persian, Hebrew, Greek, Latin, Italian and many other languages in the following centuries. Jean de La Fontaine, a French poet and fabulist (that's what a writer of fables is called) wrote many fables, some of which he acknowledged as being inspired by India's 'fables of Bidpai', an offshoot of the Panchatantra. The Indonesian version of the Panchatantra is popular as *Tantri Kamandaka*. Laos has its *Nandaka Prakarana* and Thailand has *Nang Tantrai*. The Panchatantra's influence can be seen in the 14th century English author Geoffrey Chaucer's *The Canterbury Tales*, and even in the *Br'er Rabbit* folktales of USA, which itself came from Africa. The stories from the Panchatantra have also inspired beautiful paintings including miniatures.

The Panchatantra may be the first work of literature featuring animals that speak and behave like humans. Such stories are called anthropomorphic stories. We do not know what happened to the three princes who heard all these stories. What do you think became of them?

PEPPER

How did black pepper become black? According to the legend described by 13th-century monk and teacher Bartholomaeus Anglicus, or 'Bartholomew the Englishman', the pepper seeds grew in 'the southern part of the Caucasus mountains, facing the burning heat of the sun'. He wrote in his encyclopaedia *De proprietatibus rerum* (*On the Properties of Things*) that serpents guarded the forests where the vines grew. People set fire to the forest, chasing away the snakes and leaving the peppercorns black. Do you believe this legend?

Today, if you need pepper, you just need to use the pepper shaker. No need to fight serpents, or engage in long adventures like people did centuries ago. Greek geographer Strabo (circa 64 BCE to 21 CE) wrote that the Roman Empire sent 120 ships to India to bring back many things, including pepper. The ships travelled with cargo up the Red Sea, to Berenice. From here, the cargo would be carried across the desert to the River Nile, and from there, taken on barges down the river to Alexandria. They would eventually be stored in the spice quarter of Rome.

The rich would pay heavily to buy pepper for their food. Apicius' *De re Coquinaria*, the book about cookery and dining in ancient Rome, mentioned the use of pepper in 350 recipes! Pepper was so precious that the Romans used to trade a lot of gold to take back this shrunken, black, beady spice.

Pepper is native to southern India, more specifically, the Malabar Coast. The peppercorns are the fruits of a vine from the family *Piperaceae*. Of the many varieties that grew wild, two were domesticated – the *Piper longum* or long pepper, in northeast India, and the *Piper nigrum* or black pepper in southwest India. Indian traders introduced the spice to islands in present-day Indonesia, where the vines grew well.

Indian traders had a direct link with Egypt and its market as early as 1st century BCE. Pepper definitely reached Egypt because there is hard evidence to prove it – in the well-preserved mummy of Pharaoh Ramesses II who died in 1213 BCE. By the 4th century BCE, pepper had reached Greece. In 30 BCE, when the Roman empire conquered parts of present-day Egypt, pepper was one of the things that became popular. It began to be used in the cuisine of the rich in other parts of the Roman empire including Roman Gaul (parts of present-day France and Germany). People were spending so much on pepper that Roman naturalist and philosopher, Pliny the Elder (1st century CE) complained that the Roman empire's gold was being drained by India. In 408 BCE, the cruel king Alaric of Visigoth, put the Romans in a tight spot, asking for a ransom of 5,000 pounds of gold and 3,000 pounds of pepper among other things. That was the importance given to pepper.

Explorers like Vasco da Gama dreamt of discovering easier and quicker sea routes to India so that they could monopolize the spice trade. He did reach the Malabar Coast and set up trade. The Portuguese soon destroyed the business that Alexandria, Genoa and Venice had built. When they tried to take pepper stalks to cultivate them in Portugal, King Zamorin is supposed to have said, 'You can take our pepper, but you will never be able to take our rains.' Pepper grows best in the climate specific to the coast. The spice trade from the Indian ports in the Malabar and Karavalli coasts flourished. Rani Chennabhairadevi, Jain queen of the Vijayanagara Empire in the 16th century, was called Raina-Da-Pimenta or the Queen of Pepper by the Portuguese.

The word 'pepper' may have come from the Sanskrit *pippali*. It is an important ingredient in Ayurvedic preparations. Rich in vitamins A and C, a dash of pepper in our food is good for our health. In 2025, Vietnam was the world's largest producer of pepper followed by Brazil, India, Indonesia, Cambodia and China. Our internal demand for this spice is so high that, even though we are one of the top exporters, we're also a big importer.

POLO

If you want to hear it straight from the horse's mouth, well, you can't, because Manipuri horses, like all other horses do not talk our language. But a treatise called *Kangjeirol* in the Meitei language says that horses were part of a game called *sagol kangjei* in the court of King Ningthou Kangba, the ruler of ancient Kangleipak (now Manipur) during the 14th century BCE. The first recorded or documented game happened in 33 CE. Some historians believe the game has been played since 3100 BCE.

According to Meitei mythology, the game has been played by the gods, with Marjing, the god of horses, leading it. *Sagol kangjei* from the remote and beautiful northeast of India is considered the inspiration for modern polo, played all over the world. In Meitei, *sagol* is horse, *kangjei* is stick and *kangdroom* is ball. Many versions of this game have existed. The ancient Manipuris played it sitting on the short Manipuri horses and used a long bamboo stick to steer the ball made of the wound root of the *kangkhil* creeper, also called the elephant creeper.

Nomads are believed to have played this game for entertainment and to learn the skills required for warfare in many parts of Central Asia. At times, each team would have a hundred riders! The game spread to Persia around 600 BCE, and to China in the 7th century.

The game was a favourite with the royals. Paintings depicting the game were featured in the artistic Burmese manuscripts called *parabaik*. In the 19th century, when Burma invaded Manipur, most of the region's royals fled to Assam. They resumed the play of *sagol kangjei* in their new land too.

Many hundreds of years later, British tea planters and army officers noticed the locals playing the game in Assam. The Manipuri Maharaja Sir Chandrakirti Singh is said to have introduced the game to them. A British officer is said to have exclaimed, 'We must learn the game!' And they did. They called it polo, probably after the Tibetan word for ball, *pulu*. The first official polo match was held in 1853, British East India Cavalry vs. Manipuris. The British players also formed the Silchar Kangjei Club in 1859, later called the Silchar Polo Club, making it the world's first polo club. The Calcutta Polo Club came up in 1862 and is the oldest active club in the world. The Indian Polo Association was formed in 1892.

Wherever the Britishers went, the game followed – to Malta in 1868, England in 1869, Ireland in 1870, Argentina in 1872 and Australia in 1874. The world's oldest active polo ground is Mapal Kangjeibung, in Imphal, close to the new Ebuthou Marjing Polo Complex, spread over the Marjing Hills, which includes the grazing ground for the Meitei horses. About 50 km away is another gem of Manipur, the Loktak Lake.

Polo is now played in at least 77 countries. In some places, the game is also played on elephant-back and donkey-back!

Horses and Ponies

A pony is the young of a horse is what we're taught in school. In polo, the difference between the two lies in their heights. A pony is 148 cm and under. A horse is 149 cm and above. *Meitei Sagol*, or Manipuri pony, is one of the seven recognized horse and pony breeds of India. They are known for their agility, stamina, intelligence, manoeuvrability and adaptability to the harsh climate of the region. An endangered species of Manipur, the government has now established a sanctuary in Heingang to protect and shelter the Manipuri ponies. You can see the beauty of the Meitei horse or pony, the greenery of Manipur and the grit with which the women of the land have also taken up polo in the short film, *Daughters of the Polo God*.

PYJAMA

If you're reading this in bed, maybe you're in your pyjamas. Or, some sort of what is now called loungewear. Or, home clothes. Or, to put it simply, something comfortable. Right? The word 'pyjama' comes from the Persian and Hindi words *pae* for 'leg' and *jama* for 'garment'. The pyjama was a garment that covered the legs and stayed in place with the help of a string at the waist. Because of the etymology of the word, should we infer that the pyjama was invented in India? Maybe, maybe not!

During the Kushan period (1st to 3rd century CE), there is believed to be a pyjama-like garment in use called *chalana*. The Kushan dynasty, at various points spread all the way from present-day Tajikistan and Afghanistan to Mathura in India. According to historians, pyjama-like garments called *sutala*, *pinga*, *svasthana* and *chandtika* were worn during the Gupta period (3rd to 6th century CE). The *Harshacharita*, a biography of Harshavardhana, the emperor of Kannauj, written by Banabhatta, mentions these garments. What happened to these garments, we do not know, but the Punjabi legwear called *suthan* may have come from the *svasthana*. Chinese horsemen too used to wear loose pants resembling pyjamas. Whether the garment closest to pyjamas was born in the Indian subcontinent or in Persia or in China, we do not know, but it became popular in India. It was worn along with a jama or kurta.

During the Mughal era, the rich wore intricately embroidered jamas as tops, and pyjamas that were wide and gathered around the waist and hip, ensuring that sitting down on the carpet or floor, as Indians did, would not cause an embarrassing rip in the garment. The Persian word for the garment gained ground. French traveller Jean de Thévenot, who visited parts of India in the early 1665–66, wrote how the Portuguese in Goa always wore pyjamas to bed. Indians had by now adopted the garment as a comfortable all-day wear. Unlike a dhoti, the pyjama couldn't fly away. Women started wearing it too.

William Fielding, the Earl of Denbigh, visited India and Persia in 1631, and quite liked the kurta-pyjama. With his keen interest in design (he was also the Royal Master of the Great Wardrobe), he got himself a silk set and posed for a portrait painting in this dress. The Europeans called it the 'Moghul breeches' at that time. When the British came to India, they adopted loose pyjamas and shirts as their dress for the hot afternoon naps. Made with the same soft fabric, wearing them became a bedtime routine too. They took it back to England, but it did not quite catch on there. But the Americans loved it.

By the end of the 19th century, Americans started mass producing the two-piece set and called it pajamas. Women started wearing them in the 1920s. Some designers even presented it as high-fashion beach pajamas. Actors flaunted it in the movies of the 1930s, making them even more popular. India's pyjamas had become the 'cat's pajamas', a phrase used to describe something very special. Now, the world may lounge in PJs or jammies but we in India still wear them as day-wear or as festive clothing, and of course, as nightwear too.

Cosy Coats

A gown worn when one really did not want to dress up in formal clothes – that is what came to be called a dressing gown! When the British saw Indian traders wearing a *baniyan*, they thought they could use something like that too, a loose-fitting dress that they could wear over a shirt. While the British wore pajamas at night, they lounged at home with family and close friends in a cover-all apparel called a dressing gown. Influenced also by the Japanese kimono, they got dressing gowns made in silk and other luxurious material. Later, the gowns were made with thicker material to suit the colder climes of England. That's how they came to be called house coats.

PYTHAGORAS THEOREM

If you are in middle school, you're probably learning about the Pythagoras theorem and trying to solve a problem based on it. If you're not able to crack it, take heart – thousands of mathematicians all over the world have tried to prove the theorem, because, guess what, it is believed that the Greek philosopher Pythagoras himself couldn't or did not prove it!

The theorem in geometry states that, in a right-angled triangle, the sum of the squares of the two sides is equal the square of the hypotenuse. It has many practical applications in fields such as building construction. However, thousands of years ago, what was being built with great geometric precision in India were *kund*s or 'altars' for religious rites. During the 8th century BCE, there lived in India a person called Baudhayana, who may have been a Vedic priest. He played a big part in liberating science from superstition and encouraging new thought. Apart from calculating and constructing intricate altars for *yagna*s, he also wrote all the theories and calculations that he had discovered in texts called the *Sulba Sutra*, sort of like appendices to the Vedas.

Here, he included an explanation of the relationship between the sides of a right-angled triangle. The *Sulba Sutra* has been called by internationally renowned mathematicians as possibly the oldest applied geometry text.

Pythagoras, believed to have lived between c. 570 BCE and c. 495 BCE, has remained an enigma. None of his works exist in the original. Did he really exist? Putting together information from various sources, scholars did arrive at the conclusion that he existed and travelled to many places including India in his search for knowledge. Probably the first person to call himself a 'philosopher', he learnt from several scriptures, including the Vedas. He imbibed many principles of Hinduism (refer to page 81) too, it seems, and then went back to Greece a much-enlightened man. He founded a school or monastery in Croton (now Calabria, in Italy) to share his learnings. Here, he and his students worked in secrecy on many aspects including the proof to the theorem, which came to be called the Pythagoras theorem. While no proof of the theorem exists from that period, the earliest evidence of the proof is in the work *Euclid's Elements*, composed around 300 BCE. We also have proofs worked out by the following people: Greek mathematician Pappus of Alexandria (c. 320 CE), Arab mathematician Thābit ibn Qurrah (c. 836–901 CE), Italian polymath Leonardo da Vinci (1452–1519) and the US president James Garfield (1831–1881). (Fun fact – Jim Davis, the creator of the comic strip 'Garfield' named the grumpy cat after his grandfather, who was named after this president!)

The theorem spread from India through scholars like Pythagoras, and his students who followed Pythagoreanism. His philosophy influenced famous philosophers like Plato and Aristotle who introduced these ideas to larger audiences.

Pythagoreanism also made a mark on later scientists like Nicolaus Copernicus, Johannes Kepler and Isaac Newton.

In recent times, many people think the theorem should be renamed after Baudhayana who may have been the first to write about it. But what about the wise people of Babylon who also showed that they knew something about the relationship between the sides of a right-angled triangle? They inscribed their findings on clay tablets believed to be from 1900 BCE–1600 BCE. The Babylonians called it the 'diagonal rule' since this was roughly a thousand years before the time of the mysterious Pythagoras. In the *Sulba Sutra* too, it was a mathematical fact, rather than a theorem. But a theorem by any other name is still a theorem. It all depends on which angle you see such things from, right?

QAWWALI

How wonderful it would be if there were no wars anywhere and people of different countries lived in harmony. Poets from all over the world have tried to spread the message of peace, using their words to bring people closer to one another, to make people understand each other better. Sufi poetry, born from Islam, is one such devotional practice that urges us to look within ourselves and to realize that we are all one. Sufi verses are called *qual* in Persian.

The roots of qawwali are in ancient Persia. Sufi saints and their followers used to practice *sama*, the recitation and mindful listening of verses, every evening. In the 11th century, a major migration of people happened, and *sama* became known in Turkey, Uzbekistan and the Indian subcontinent. There is a charming story about how *sama* gave birth to qawwali.

Amir Khusrau was a 13th- to 14th-century poet and Sufi follower in Delhi. He wrote in Persian, Punjabi and Hindavi, a dialect of Hindi spoken at that time. He lived in Delhi and was the disciple of Hazrat Nizamuddin Auliya. Once when his mentor was very sad, Khusrau decided he needed to do something to make him happy. So, he took a set of Sufi verses, tweaked them to make them simpler to follow and set them to music. While Dhrupad was the formal style of music of those times, he decided to make that simpler too to reflect the music of the common people. The result was a set of *qual* arranged in a beautiful and easy-to-follow musical composition. It came to be called qawwali. Over time, Amir Khusrau 'Dehlavi' came to be known as the 'Father of Qawwali'.

A qawwali group may have anywhere from eight to fifteen members, including one or two lead singers, a few background singers, a chorus and musicians playing on the harmonium, tabla, dholak and the sarangi. The energetic performance gains momentum as both the singers and the audience clap rhythmically to the music, since qawwals believe that the body too is a musical instrument.

In India, the Ajmer Sharif Dargah is a beloved place for people of all faiths. It was built in honour of Sufi saint Khwaja Moinuddin Chishti, a scholar from Persia who settled down in Ajmer, Rajasthan, in the 12th to 13th century. The Ajmer Urs each year attracts thousands of devotees. Qawwalis are performed with great reverence here.

The work of Sufi poets Jalal ad-Din Muhammad Rumi, Amir Khusrau, Bulleh Shah and Baba Farid are most often picked up for qawwalis. One of the world's leading qawwal, as the singers are called, was Nusrat Fateh Ali Khan. He was born into a family of qawwals in Pakistan that had practised this art of devotional music for over six hundred years. He had a huge fan following not just in Pakistan and India, but all over the world too. He was a great advocator of peace between countries and performed in many countries.

For some reason, qawwals are usually male. Prabha Bharti was India's first female qawwal. Children too are drawn to qawwalis. Look up the energetic performance called 'Annt Bahar' by the Qawwali Kids (Jodhpur) online. Maybe, you and your friends could perform a qawwali for a special day in school?

Sufi Sounds

At the Dargah of Nizamuddin Auliya, also called Hazrat Nizamuddin Dargah in New Delhi, qawwali is performed every day. This Sufi place of worship is open to people of all faiths. Some of the other famous places where you can experience the magic of qawwali are the Yousufain Dargah in Hyderabad, Dargah Hazrat Salim Chishti in Fatehpur Sikri, Agra, Ajmer Sharif Dargah, Ajmer, and Haji Ali Dargah, Mumbai.

RAIN GAUGE

How much rain do you think your city or town receives? Too much? Too little? A lot? Or, maybe, if you live in the Atacama Desert, you would say, 'Rain? What's that?' because it hasn't rained there in four hundred years! These answers make for good conversation about the weather. But if you were a farmer, you would need more scientific data about rainfall. You'd, in fact, be very happy to have a rain gauge.

In ancient India, around 400 BCE, rain measuring instruments were made so that the administers could calculate how much tax farmers had to pay to the king. If they had farms that received good rains, they had to pay a higher tax. If farms received less rain, the farmers had to pay a smaller tax. The amount of rainfall also helped the supervisors to advise farmers on what seeds were to be sown and when.

While a similar rainfall measurement practice may also have existed in ancient Greece earlier to this, the first known mention of it is in the *Arthashastra*. This is the Sanskrit text about governance credited to Chanakya. Under the section on building construction, it mentions that a *varshamana*, a bowl as wide as an 'aratni' (roughly equal to 457 mm), should be kept out to measure the rainfall.

A rainfall measuring system was next mentioned in the *Mishnah*, a record of Jewish life between 2nd century BCE and 2nd century CE in Palestine. For nearly a thousand years after that, there does not seem to be any record of rainfall measurement. The next mention is in the *Shushu Jiuzhang*, a mathematical treatise in nine parts, compiled in China in 1247 CE. Around this time, most places in Asia also started measuring rainfall.

The first standardized rain gauge called the *cheuguge*, was invented in Korea, by King Sejong in 1441. Almost two hundred years after that, Italian scientist Benedetto Castelli, a student of Galileo, made the first graduated instrument to measure rainfall. In 1662, English architect Christopher Wren, famous for having redesigned London's St. Paul's Cathedral, invented the tilting rain gauge that could measure hourly rainfall in a place. It was modified later by his friend and fellow scientist Robert Hooke in 1679 as a 'weather clock'.

Rainfall data is needed not just to help farmers plan their work, but also to calculate flood forecasts and to operate hydro-power stations and regulate reservoirs. Did ancient India's rainfall gauge inspire the later inventions? We don't know. As a largely agricultural country, rainfall measurement is very important to us.

Make Your Own Rain Gauge

- Take a clear plastic bottle, cut the top so that it makes a funnel when upturned.
- Using a scale, mark the bottle starting 5 cm above the base. Draw evenly spaced markings in millimetres above this point.
- Place a few small stones inside the bottle at the base so that it stands firm. Pour water into the bottle up to the 0 mark you have made.
- Place the funnel on the bottle. Your rain gauge is ready!

When it rains next, place it on the terrace or in any other open place where the rain falls directly from the sky. Record the time. Check the water level exactly an hour later to see how many millimetres of rain your location has received. Enough to demand hot pakodas while listening to your favourite songs?

ROCK EDICTS

An edict is a proclamation of a ruler, or government, or a person of authority, displayed for everyone to see. Something like your school principal's new rule about no ragging put up on the notice board. While ancient people all over the world wrote or drew something on clay, or on walls in caves, they did not write entire lists of the ideal code of conduct. Ashoka, the king of the Mauryas, was the first in the Indian subcontinent to get his edicts carved into rocks and polished sandstone pillars in the 3rd century BCE. While there is evidence of much older rock inscriptions like the ones in Sinai Peninsula, or those of Darius I, the third king of the Achaemenid Empire on a cliff at Mount Behistun in present-day Iran, the Ashokan Edicts are the first ones about moral conduct, the first ones about social welfare.

Kalinga was a kingdom in the eastern coast of India, in present-day Odisha. It was a trading partner of the Mauryan kingdom. It is not clear why, but Ashoka waged war on the Kalingas, killing thousands of them. When he looked at the dead and wounded on the battlefield in 261 BCE, he had a massive change of heart and vowed to never be violent. He embraced Buddhism and, through that religion, became a strong advocator of non-violence. He started following *dhamma*, a moral code of conduct. In Prakrit, by *dhamma* he meant 'goodness, in terms of personal qualities as well as behaviour towards all living things'. The Sanskrit equivalent for the word was *dharma*. The edicts were written in the Brahmi script, using Prakrit dialects.

To ensure that everyone in his vast land from present-day Afghanistan to Bangladesh, and almost all of India except Kerala and Tamil Nadu were informed about *dhamma*, he got the notes inscribed on rocks and pillars. These are called Ashoka's Edicts. Over 30 edicts have been found in places as far-flung as Kandahar (Afghanistan), Shahbazgarhi (Pakistan), Kalsi (Uttarakhand), Girnar (Gujarat), Yerragundi (Andhra Pradesh), Sopara (Maharashtra), Jaugada (Odisha) and Lumbini (Nepal). Inscribed on horizontal rock faces and vertical ones, he had them placed on caravan routes and places that got maximum exposure – much like present-day hoardings.

The edicts show how full of repentance the king was for having gone to war and killing people. Referring to himself as Devanampriya ('beloved of the gods') in the edicts, he asked his subjects, who he considered to be his children, to take care of their teachers and elders. If the edicts were converted into pithy sayings for today's citizens, it would read something like this:

Be kind to animals.

Do not harm plants and animals in the wild.

Speak the truth.

Be tolerant towards all religions.

Win through dialogue and compassion, not through war.

The edicts have been categorized as minor rock edicts, minor pillar edicts, major rock edicts and major pillar edicts. The ones in the north and east are written in Magadhi Prakrit in the Brahmi script, while the ones in the northwest are written in Prakrit, Greek and Aramaic. The Shahbazgarhi edit is written right to left, in the Kharosthi script. Not content with educating his own subjects, Ashoka sent missionaries to China, Thailand, Sri Lanka and Greece to spread the lessons of non-violence and compassion.

The influence of Ashoka's edicts was felt far beyond the boundaries of his kingdom. Even though the edicts were not meant to preach Buddhism, they helped in the spread of the religion far and wide.

Many compositions created in early civilizations have not survived in their original form. Ashoka's edicts are carved in stone, untarnished and clear, from the minute they were etched 2,300 years ago, informing the world to stop war and love all.

Talk About Over-Writing!

Gupta kings loved to have inscriptions on coins. They also had inscriptions on pillars. The Allahabad Pillar inside the Prayagraj Fort on the banks of the Yamuna is believed to have been commissioned by the Mauryan king Ashoka in around 232 BCE. This sandstone pillar has some of his edicts, and some by his queen Karuvaki. In the 4th century CE, the Gupta king Samudragupta had the same pillar inscribed with words about his own greatness. Mughal emperor Jahangir had his genealogical details inscribed in Persian, in a beautiful *nastaliq* script. If you now have the urge to scribble something on the pillar, beware! It is guarded by the military, and you need permission to view it.

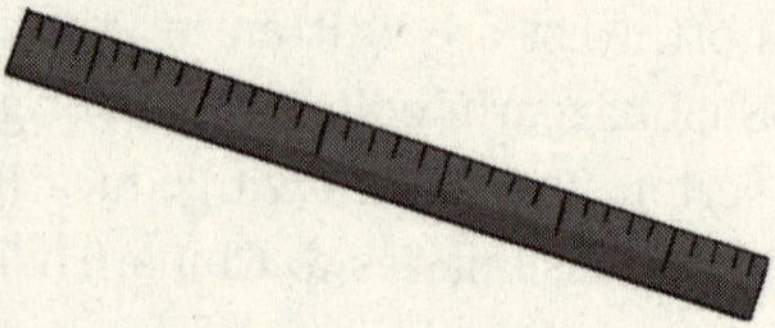

RULER

When you're flipping your plastic scale or ruler in geometry class next time, look at it closely. What is the distance between any two consecutive bars?

In 1930–31, English archaeologist Ernest Mackay found a fragment of shell in Mohenjo-daro which, after close examination, he called a 'measure of length'. It was one of the world's earliest measuring scales. While scales were found in other civilizations too, this one showed extremely accurate divisions. Imagine specific shells being brought from the Arabian Sea to workshops where they were converted into beads, household tools, spindles and other things! The Mohenjo-daro scale would have required the use of strong bronze chisels. The fractured 'measure of length' is preserved at the National Museum, New Delhi.

A ruler made of ivory was found in Lothal which is marked to measure one-sixteenth of an inch. That's less than 2 mm. The only other linear scale found in an Indus site is a tiny bronze rod with four divisions. The incredible civil engineering skills as seen from the ruins of the IVC couldn't have been achieved without a set of standard measuring tools. From the excavations done so far, rulers have been rare, suggesting that there may have been other means to measure length.

SAREE

If there is one apparel that is immediately recognized anywhere in the world as Indian, it is the saree, or sari. But in reality, the saree belongs to the Indian subcontinent which includes Pakistan, Bangladesh, Sri Lanka and Nepal. The earliest evidence of the use of a saree-like clothing dates back to the IVC. Excavations from IVC sites, especially Mehrgarh in present-day Pakistan, show figurines draped in a saree-like cloth. Cotton was already being cultivated and woven into cloth during that period. By ancient definition, the saree is 'a piece of unstitched cloth' – a really long piece, anywhere from 3.5 yards to 9 yards.

The *paridhana* mentioned in the Rig Veda and the Prakrit word *sattika* in Buddhist texts may refer to handwoven saree-like attire. During the Vedic period, the saree became associated with religious culture. The saree was one piece of cloth that served both as topwear and bottomwear. This appeared to be the case even during the Sangam period (3rd century BCE to 3rd century CE). By the Gupta period (320 CE–550 CE), sarees of gold and silk came into being. During the Mughal era (1526–1857), sarees became brighter with jewel tones, had more floral patterns and became a thing of beauty and luxury.

With Mahatma Gandhi's call to all Indians to join the Swadeshi Movement, women started wearing khadi sarees. Among them was a British lady called Madeleine Slade who was very active in the Indian freedom movement. Given the name Mirabehn by Gandhiji, she took to wearing khadi sarees. Meanwhile social reformer and sister-in-law of the Nobel laureate Rabindranath Tagore, Jnanadanandini Debi wanted to retain her Indian look even while attending British events with her husband, Satyendranath Tagore. But the British officers at that time looked down upon the saree. By pairing the saree with smart, English-style blouses and adding a Parsi touch to the drape, she invented a modern way that no one could find fault with. That style, the closest to what most women wear in India is called the *Nivi* style.

As Indian women settled down in different parts of the world, the saree became a well-recognized garment. Sarees were and continue to be a large canvas to showcase India's various brilliant textile craftwork. Each region of India has a heritage design of its own. By the way, not all 'unstitched' costumes are sarees. For example, women in Manipur wear *phanek-innaphi*, a traditional two-piece set and in Kerala, some women wear *mundum neriyathum*.

SEAMLESS CELESTIAL GLOBE

Shall we try something? Close your eyes. Imagine you're sitting on a hill on a dark starry night. Imagine the sky as a transparent layer all around the Earth. Now, try to pinpoint which star is where in that globular sky. No, you can't use a sky-view app. Got it? Or tough? In the days when sailors depended on calculations based on the apparent position of stars to decide which way to steer their ship, they used a device called an astrolabe. A celestial sphere was a teaching and demonstration tool used to help astrolabists. It was not accurate, but it was a great help. You could call it a 3D model of the sky visualized as a hollow globe around Earth. Since stars are so far away from us, they each look equally far from us, even though they are not. The metallic, hollow globes had inscriptions of stars and constellations on the outside, as a mirror image of what we would see if we were inside the globe.

While many celestial globes are still found in museums across the world, seamless celestial globes are rare. Making such seamless spheres was a work of genius, something known to only a few metallurgists of Mughal India. If you've noticed the globe in your geography class, or a rubber ball, you may have noticed that there is a seam running along the circumference, where the two halves of the sphere are sealed. But during the Mughal rule in India, celestial globes cast in brass had no seams.

This discovery was made by science historian, Emilie Savage-Smith, after she was asked to examine an undated celestial globe that had come into the possession of the National Museum of History and Technology (now renamed National Museum of American History), a part of the Smithsonian Museum in Washington, D.C., USA. The globe showed 48 constellations. What she discovered surprised metallurgists all over the world – it was a seamless metal globe. The globe sent her on a 10-year study of not just globes but also how science and astronomy developed in the world. After travelling all over the world to study more than 100 existing celestial globes, she found that all of them reflected the same culture of Islamdom, whether they were made in India or Spain, whether made by Muslims or non-Muslims, whether they were inscribed in Arabic, Persian or Sanskrit.

The earliest known seamless celestial sphere is believed to have been cast in Kashmir by Ali Kashmiri ibn Luqman in 1589–90 CE during the reign of Akbar. How did he manage this seemingly impossible feat? He used a method called lost-wax casting or *cire perdue*. The globe carries a message from him, saying he made it as a memory aid for astrolabe makers. A workshop in Lahore, also under Akbar's rule at that time, was most well-known for metallurgy work and the manufacture of astrolabes and hollow brass spheres.

A celestial globe made by Muhammad Salih Tatawi in 1663–64 CE has the names of constellations and his signature in both Arabic and Sanskrit. He is believed to have been knowledgeable of both the Arabic–Islamic and Hindu schools of astronomy.

In 1842, Lala Balhumal Lahuri, a Hindu maker of precision instruments made a globe, inscribed in Arabic and Persian, for his Sikh patron. Talk about cultural unity! Can they be made today? Technically impossible, is the consensus.

The seamless celestial globes that travelled from Mughal India to the rest of the world continue to make viewers go all starry-eyed.

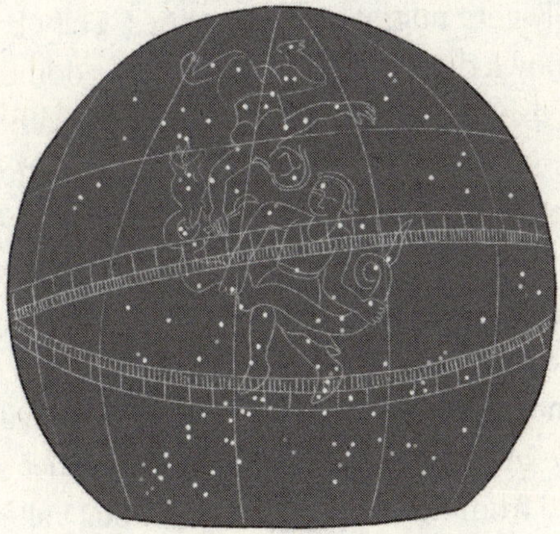

SESAME OIL

The population of IVC cities kept growing as more and more villagers migrated to the cities. They brought with them the knowledge they had gained, like domestication of many crops like sesame, cotton and peas. Sesame (*Sesamum indicum*), also called gingelly is one of the most ancient oilseed crop. While the origin of sesame was debated – India or Africa? – for over a century, now it is widely accepted that it originated in the Indian subcontinent. It was cultivated especially for its oil. The earliest discovery of its use is from Harappa in the IVC somewhere between 2700–1900 BCE. With available evidence, the hypothesis among scientists is that sesame was domesticated from wild varieties in the Indus Valley.

By the end of the third millennium BCE, it is believed that trade routes from Harappa helped the seeds reach Mesopotamia. By the second millennium BCE, it had reached Egypt.

Sesame oil was exported from the Gulf of Cambay and shipped to both Arabia and Africa. From here it was shipped to the Roman Empire. In the famous story of *Ali Baba and the Forty Thieves*, Morgiana kills the thieves with hot oil. Could that be sesame oil? The story does feature the magic phrase 'Open Sesame'.

SEWAGE SYSTEM

In the 21st century, with all the advancement we have made in science and engineering, our cities are still struggling with maintaining sewage systems – the networks of pipes that take away waste material from homes, offices, parks and other buildings through channels. However, the IVC had one of the earliest sewage systems in the world. The other was in the Minoan civilization in the Mediterranean island of Crete.

Excavations in IVC sites have revealed houses made with mud and clay bricks, with most houses having a bathroom. Even though the toilets were just pits, the waste would go out through drains that led to the city sewers. The drains were built with tightly packed bricks to give the waste a smooth flow out of the house and into cesspits. Each house had a well, with many of them having a hand-operated system to draw water. This water could be poured into the toilet to 'flush' the poop. There were also public baths like the Great Bath of Mohenjo-daro, that had a well-connected system to store water. All this, 4,000 years ago!

It was only two thousand years later that the Roman civilization and others had sanitation of the same level of sophistication.

How did the sanitation genius of the IVC influence other civilizations? We do not know yet. But, ever since the rediscovery of Indus sites, excavations and research continue because no waste matter is really a waste. Scientists can now study specimens from ancient sites to discover a whole lot about our ancient civilizations and apply the learnings to the present and future. You can learn a lot about the sanitation systems of the world at the Sulabh International Museum of Toilets in New Delhi.

SHAMPOO

If you're shopping for a shampoo in a supermarket, your head may reel just looking at the number of brands and sub-brands on offer. Stay cool. Don't let decision-making get to the roots of your hair! Instead, you could walk to the groceries department and pick up some *shikakai* (*Acacia concinna*), amla and soapnuts (*Sapindus*, from the Latin word '*sapo*' for soap and '*indicus*' for from India). Go home, boil them together in water, filter and bottle the liquid once it is cooled. Use this as your shampoo. Those are the ingredients the ancient Indians of the IVC used over 4,000 years ago.

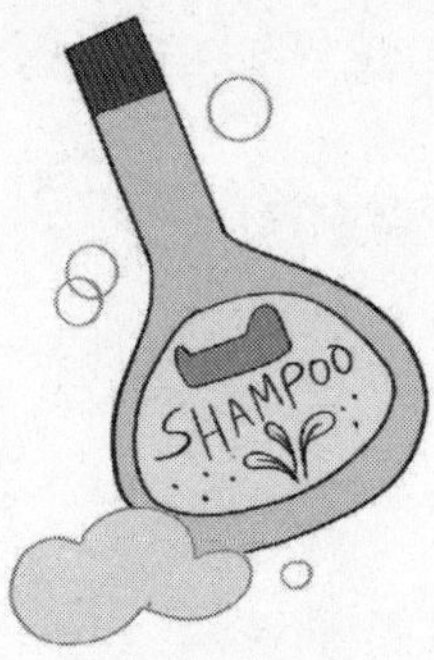

While soaps had a long and not so clean history (you'll find it in *Travelling Treasures: 100 Incredible Tales of How Things Came to India*) and were being used to wash hair too, it was only in the mid-eighteenth century that the word 'shampoo' was used in English. It came from the Hindi word 'chāmpo' from *champna*, roughly meaning 'to

smear, knead and massage', which probably came from the Sanskrit word *chapayati*. In 1814, Sake Dean Mahomed, a British Indian traveller and surgeon, and his Irish wife Jane Daly introduced the concept of 'shampooing vapour bath' to England by setting up a salon.

In a world flooded with commercial shampoos, the shampoo recipe from the IVC is still keeping heads and hair strong and shining, all around the world!

SHIPBUILDING

We don't know who first thought of using a boat or a floating object that one could sit on and ride on water. We don't know if prehistoric – meaning, the time before recorded history – seafarers used some object to move around the islands of Sundaland, east of the Indian peninsula. However, we do know that the oldest images of boats were found on Egyptian vases that are at least 6,000 years old. These narrow boats may have been made with papyrus reeds.

What we also know is that Indian shipbuilders were highly skilled. When Alexander the Great had to return home with his army, he is believed to have commissioned the building of 1,800 ships. Remember, this was in 326 BCE when production lines and factories did not exist. During the Mauryan era in 321 BCE, Kautilya's *Arthashastra* mentions *navadhyaksha* or a superintendent of shipping. This and other such mentions indicate the importance of shipping during those times. *Yuktikalpataru*, believed to be a text composed by King Bhoja of Dhara, talks about the connection between architecture and the cosmos. This too mentions the many kinds of ships or boats made for different purposes. Did these texts have easy DIY instructions to help other shipbuilders? No. You see, these may have been seen as trade secrets and so they stayed undocumented. Shipbuilders taught their wards the art and techniques, and thus the knowledge was passed down from generation to generation.

As early as the 2nd century BCE, Indians were known to build strong boats that were strong enough to be navigated across to the Red Sea in the west or to the South China Sea in the east, and return. The biggest of the ships could carry over 1,000 people. Large artefacts carved out of Indian ivory like mirrors, furniture and boxes would be loaded on these ships. Animals like rhinoceroses, tigers and leopards too were transported on these huge ships to ports in the Red Sea, from where they were taken to Rome and other cities.

In the 14th century, an Italian monk called Friar Odoric wrote with wonder about India's huge ships that could each carry 700 people. Thousands of India-built ships criss-crossed the Indian Ocean helping with international trade. Admiral Zheng He, who headed the Chinese fleet of ships in the early 15th century, is believed to have sent his chronicler Ma Huan to study the shipbuilding process in Bengal. The Portuguese were so impressed with the shipbuilders in the Konkan and other western coastal regions of India that they called them Mestre – Portuguese for 'master craftsperson'.

The 5th-century painting on a rock wall in the Ajanta Caves shows a unique ship. A stitched ship. Yes, stitched. With ropes made of coir and dipped with fish oil. Coir ropes were threaded through precision holes drilled into wooden planks in intricate patterns that were not only pretty but very practical. They held the ship together and were most suited for the weather on the Indian Ocean. In the Harappan site of Lothal, Gujarat, archaeologists found the wreckage of a ship made with Kerala timber. This was a stitched ship.

Harappan seals featuring ships, and terracotta seals in West Bengal's Bangarh and Chandraketugarh featuring vessels at sea have also been found by archaeologists.

In 2025, the Indian Navy, the Ministry of Culture and a company in Goa collaborated to rebuild a stitched ship based on the Ajanta painting. It travelled from the Indian coast to Oman.

SNAKES AND LADDERS

If you remember the excitement of climbing a really tall slide in the park, you may also remember the rush of air and thrill you would feel as you slide down. What goes up – you – must come down, right? In the case of a slide, it is pure fun. But when you're playing snakes and ladders, coming down isn't a great feeling, is it? Thankfully, you can roll the dice and expect to climb up a ladder again. One of the things that this ancient game teaches us is to learn to take the good with the bad.

The early versions of the game in India were known by different names like *moksha patam*, *gyan chaupar*, *gyan bazi* and *pachisi*. Nepal had a version called *nagapasa* meaning snake-dice. The board game that is now played almost all over the world may have begun its journey in India, maybe 2,000 years ago. A more popular belief is that the Marathi saint Jnaneshwar, also known as Dnyandev, who lived during the 13th century invented the game of *moksha patam* or *paramapadam*. Some people also interpret the text in a 10th-century Jain work called *Rishabh Panchasika* written in Prakrit to believe that the game may have been played in the 10th century.

Rather than for recreation, the game was designed to teach people the value of virtues. The idea was to teach the philosophy of attaining moksha or moving towards the Almighty, or reaching heaven by following a virtuous path and avoiding bad habits or vices. In all the versions, some squares had virtues inscribed on them, like generosity, reliability, knowledge and truthfulness. A board, dating back to the 19th century, a board carried inscriptions with ideas from Islamic and Sufi spiritual beliefs. In this way, the game was used by people of different faiths, to establish a similar viewpoint – the importance of taking the righteous path.

Some squares were marked with vices like greed, disobedience, anger, arrogance and vanity. The squares were drawn or painted on cloth or paper. Some were intricately painted with striking borders. The one preserved at the National Museum, New Dehi, has the playing area designed like a Rajasthani fort. The number of squares differed – 72 squares in the Hindu version, 84 in the Jain version, and 300 in a 'Punjab Hills' version. (In the art world, Punjab Hills refers to the geographical area of the foothills of the Himalayas, mostly in present-day Jammu and Himachal Pradesh, and the art produced in the royal kingdoms of Kangra, Kullu, Mandi, Mankot and others.) The numbers were written in a boustrophedon – alternate lines reading left to right and right to left – with squares inscribed with a virtue or a vice. The player rolled the dice or cowrie shells and depending on the count, they moved their

piece ahead. If they came to a vice, a snake would bring them down. If they landed on a virtue they would move forward or up a ladder.

In the 1890s, the game became popular in Victorian England. While the English board retained some virtues and vices, it dropped the religious and spiritual values of the game and made it a simple game of chance for recreation. It began to be called snakes and ladders. The Indian versions had more snakes than ladders to signify that there are more vices that can bring down a person than virtues to redeem them. The English board had equal number of snakes and ladders. The game brought families together, did not need any particular skill and could be played by people of all ages.

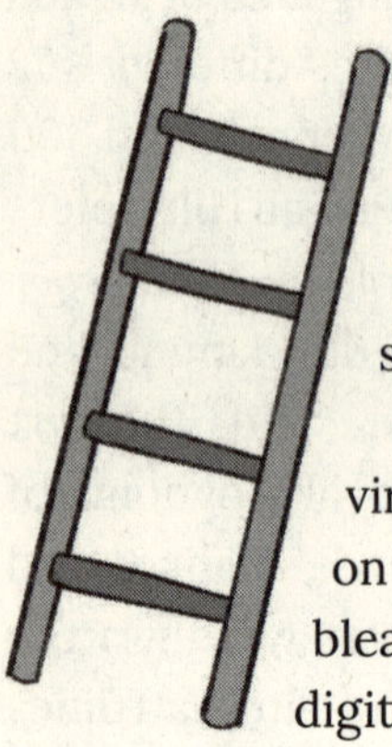

In 1943, the game went through a major change when it was introduced to the United States of America as 'chutes and ladders'. The manufacturers thought having snakes in a game would make it scary for children.

Now, is playing snakes and ladders a virtue or vice? A virtue for sure, if you play on a physical board, and maybe a cause for bleary eyes if you get hooked playing it on a digital app.

SUGAR CULTIVATION

Mary Poppins made 'a spoonful of sugar' very popular in modern times with her song. If she had lived over 3,000 years ago, she may have sung, 'a cane-full of sugar makes the teeth very strong' or something like that. You see, the idea of squeezing out sugar from the cane was found out by ancient Indians only around 3,000 years ago. While there is no archaeological evidence to prove when and where sugar was first grown, many pointers are that it happened in New Guinea about 10,000 years back. The idea of cultivating sugarcane (*Saccharum officinarum*) moved eastwards through the Pacific Ocean to Solomon Islands and Polynesia. It also moved westwards to Indonesia, Philippines and North India. The grass with long, strong sweet canes grew well, and people chomped happily on the canes to draw the sweet juice.

When Indians began squeezing out the canes and started producing sugar, the demand for the sweet material increased. The ability to change cane juice into grains of sugar was a huge discovery. The process was kept a secret, and trade in sugar kept Indian rulers rich. Chroniclers in Alexander's army, in 326 BCE, wrote about 'stones' that were sweeter than figs and honey. These are believed to be the hard sugar which were later called *khand* and gave rise to *khandi*. Want to guess what this gave rise to? Candy, anyone? The fact that sugar is called *chini* in Hindi and many other Indian languages may indicate that ancient China may have had a hand in purifying sugar. According to Chinese documents, at least two teams came from China to India around 647 CE to study the process. That brown sugar is called *misri* (also what Egypt was called) may indicate that Egypt too had a role in the production of sugar outside India.

Around 518 BCE, Darius I, the ruler of the Persian Achaemenid Empire conquered parts of the Indus Valley, up to the Jhelum River. The Persians took the knowledge of making sugar from here and started producing their own. Sugar became an important part of their trade with Europe.

The cultivation in Persia continued for a thousand years. Called 'Persian reed', it was introduced to Egypt around 710 CE. From here, the Arab traders took it to Cyprus, Crete and Sicily by the 9th century. Production did not take off in a big way until a few centuries later. In the 15th century, the Portuguese started taking control of sugar production. Portuguese prince, Henry the Navigator, introduced the cane to Madeira in 1425. By the late 15th century, production boomed in this archipelago, making it the biggest producer of refined sugar. By 1510, however, because of several reasons including deforestation, production declined drastically.

In 1493, Christopher Colombus carried sugarcane seedlings to Hispaniola, an island in the West Indies. In the 17th century, sugar became one of the most wanted and traded substances in the world. What followed is not a great commentary on humanity. Countries were colonized. Slaves were traded and made to work on sugarcane fields under inhuman conditions. Slavery was abolished in the

19th century. Another system came up – the indentured labour system. This involved labourers 'voluntarily' appearing before a judge to say that they were willing to work abroad. Millions of Indian workers were forced to be part of this system and had to settle in plantations in British colonies abroad. The system that was set up for sugarcane production continued in the plantations of coffee, cotton, cocoa, rubber and tea.

During the British rule in India, sugar consumption went up so much that sugar had to be imported from places like Mauritius. In 2026, India is the second largest producer of sugar. Sugar may be one of the least expensive forms of energy-giving food, but remember, overeating sugar may not only cause a sugar-high and subsequent crash but also damage your teeth – and the treatment of that can be quite expensive!.

THE JUNGLE BOOK

Would you want to live in a jungle with a black panther and a jolly bear? British author Rudyard Kipling created a whole new world for children and adults featuring a little boy called Mowgli, who grows up in the care of mother wolf Raksha and her family, the panther Bagheera and the bear Baloo. It has entertained many generations of readers and viewers. The author was born in Bombay in 1865, in the Sir J.J. School of Arts campus where his father taught architectural sculpture.

Rudyard Kipling was greatly inspired by India. In his autobiography *Something of Myself*, he wrote how his Goan-Portuguese nanny used to take him and his sister to the markets and how he loved the sights and sounds of India. But they were shipped off to England when he was a little boy, to stay with caretakers, not a happy experience for him and his little sister at all. He returned to India as a seventeen-year-old, and grew up to be a journalist and poet, but his years spent away from home affected him a lot. He must have gone through confusing emotions about his own identity – like, was he an Indian in England? An English boy in India? Which was home? Unknowingly, he showed these thoughts through the character of Mowgli in short stories that were published in magazines between 1893 and 1894. A collection of these stories was published in 1894 as *The Jungle Book*. Mowgli first appeared in a story called 'In the Rukh'. *The Second Jungle Book*, with more stories was published in 1895.

The stories are anthropomorphic – that means, the animals in them talk and think like humans. Were they inspired by the Panchatantra and Jataka Tales? By his own admission, Kipling was inspired by many things – for example, the lions he saw in South Africa, and a story he read about a Zulu prince befriending a wolf called Galazi. Kipling wrote the stories while living not in India, not in England, but in Vermont, USA.

Does the Seeonee Hills of the book really exist? The name may have come from the town of Seoni, near present-day Pench Tiger Reserve, and the jungle setting may be closer to that of the Kanha Tiger Reserve and the ruins described in the book may be similar to the Bandhavgarh Tiger Reserve. While these reserves were once a continuous forest in the Satpura Range, Kipling's first draft was set in the Aravalli Hills, or the present-day Aravalli Range. Do authors actually visit the places they write about? Not necessarily. Kipling himself never visited Seoni and got all the information he needed from other books about it, including a scholarly book written by his father John Lockwood Kipling. His father also illustrated the early stories of *The Jungle Book* along with W.H. Drake and Paul Frenzeny.

While the Mowgli story is the most well-known, *The Jungle Book* also includes the wonderful stories of Rikki-Tikki-Tavi the mongoose, Darzee the tailorbird and many other characters. So popular was the book that it was made into a film in 1942. Since then, many movie versions of *The Jungle Book* have been made by many people including Walt Disney.

Apart from the movies, do you know one more important phenomenon inspired by *The Jungle Book*? The Cub Scout Movement, with its rules written in *The Wolf Cub's Handbook*. Robert Baden-Powell, who started the Boy Scout Movement and later the Girl Scout Movement, was a good friend of Rudyard Kipling. Now, when you see Col Hathi and his gang marching onscreen to 'Hup, two, three, four, KEEP IT UP!' you may be able to see how our country inspired millions of children across the world over several generations.

TOOLS MADE OF ERNESTITE

Bead-making was a popular craft of the Indus Valley Civilization. That they were traded and much in demand in the elite societies of the world is also well-known. The beads were made of soft stones like limestone, steatite and lapis lazuli at first. Later beads were made with hard stones like chert, agate and jasper. Ancient Gujarat was rich in agate resources, attracting bead makers to the region. But how were holes drilled in these stones? With a tool that had a drill bit harder than agate, of course. When Ernest J.H. Mackay was in charge of the excavations at Chanhu-daro, an IVC settlement in present-day Pakistan, archaeologists found drill bits made of an unknown stone. They named the stone ernestite after their boss. It was known only much later that ernestite was a synthetic stone engineered by the Harappans. To produce the stone, they used sand and laterite-rich clays and sintered them at precisely 1100 degree centigrade! Other than Harappa and Mohenjo-daro in present-day Pakistan, ernestite stones have also been found in the IVC sites in Gujarat such as Dholavira, Kanmer, Khirsara, Bhagatrav, Bagasara, Shikarpur and Nagwada.

TURMERIC

In 1995, the US Patent and Trademark Office issued a patent for the wound-healing properties of turmeric. Reading the news in India, the then director of Council of Scientific and Industrial Research (CSIR), Dr Raghunath Mashelkar was flabbergasted. How could a patent be given to knowledge that had been in public domain for thousands of years? Backed by the government of India, and CSIR, he challenged the patent claim. After 14 months, the patent was revoked in 1997, a major win for a country fighting for traditional knowledge. India set up the Traditional Knowledge Digital Library to avoid biopiracy and to give free access to ancient knowledge to everyone interested in it.

Turmeric (*Curcuma longa*) is native to South India and Indonesia. The part of the plant that we use is a rhizome, an underground stem. Turmeric and ginger belong to the *Zingiberaceae* family (and cardamom too. More about that on page 38). Turmeric is used as a spice, food preservative and colouring agent. Its most important role is in the preparation of traditional medicine in Ayurveda, Unani medicine, Tibetan medicine and Chinese medicine. Indus

Valley excavations and cuneiform scrolls from 7th century BCE show evidence of the use of turmeric.

Turmeric was also listed in the Tang-era *Materia Medica*, compiled in China in 659 CE. Though turmeric is made up of many compounds, it is the curcumin that is responsible for most of its medicinal properties. Turmeric is called the golden spice in English, *terra merita* (meritorious earth) in Latin, and in Sanskrit *haridra* is one of its 53 names! When Marco Polo found the plant, he claimed that it had all the characteristics of saffron but was a root (you mean, rhizome, Signore Polo). So, of course, turmeric's fancy name is Indian saffron.

The rhizome was carried on the Silk Road to Antioch (now Antakya, in Türkiye) around 300 BCE when it was an important city in ancient Greece. It also went from India's west coast to southern Arabia, moving from there onto the ancient Incense Route – the web of trade routes from southern Arabia to the traders in Egypt, Rome and Mesopotamia.

Over time, people discovered that turmeric had a host of beneficial properties. Let's get out the big words that describe it – antibacterial, antiviral, anti-inflammatory, antitumor, antioxidant, antiseptic, cardioprotective and digestive properties. So the next time you think there's too much turmeric in your curry (What's that? Page 61), or someone asks you to gulp a hot glass of pepper-turmeric milk to cure your cough, just be thankful and enjoy it. India's golden spice is now considered a superfood. It is spicing up international beverages and being called turmeric latte in fancy places.

There are many kinds of turmeric. Lakadong turmeric from Meghalaya's Jaintia Hills has the highest percentage of curcumin. Alleppey, Erode and Sangli are the other places that produce valuable turmeric. India produces 80 per cent of the world's turmeric. It is also the largest consumer and exporter. Guess which two countries outside the Indian subcontinent consume the most turmeric as a staple spice? Ethiopia and Eritrea, both in Africa.

UNIVERSITY – NALANDA

Nalanda Mahavihara, or the ancient university of Nalanda, was founded in 427 CE, in Magadha (modern-day Bihar). It was more a monastery than what we now call a university. Yet, it is recognized as the oldest residential university in the world because it brought teachers and students together to study and learn different subjects. For 800 years, it welcomed students from all over the world. With its grand library with nine million books, it was where seekers of knowledge exchanged ideas, had deep discussions and serious debates. The subjects here included mathematics, astrology, astronomy, medicine, logic and Buddhism. Ayurveda was also taught here. Many Buddhists believe that the source of all Buddhist knowledge came from Nalanda. The management principles first set up at Nalanda are the ones that many universities still follow – large libraries, comfortable living quarters, encouragement to free and fair learning, tolerance towards diverse thoughts, acceptance to students from different countries and encouragement to exchange and share knowledge.

Nalanda Mahavihara was founded by the Gupta emperor Kumaragupta I as a Buddhist monastery even though he followed Hinduism. Many other Indian and Javanese (ethnic group in Indonesia) philanthropists supported the running of the university. Funds were set up for specific projects, one of them being to support scholars from China. Thus, scholars who studied at Nalanda took home the culture and knowledge of India to different places in Asia. The inscriptions found at the ruins tells of people who gifted entire villages to the university.

Aryabhata, the man who gave zero to the world is believed to have headed the university in the 6th century. His work made a huge contribution to the development of mathematical and astronomical concepts in the Arabian world. The university regularly supported student exchange programmes so that scholars from Nalanda could go to China, Korea, Japan, Sri Lanka and Indonesia, not only to spread Buddhism but also to share knowledge about other subjects.

Around 1190, many believe that Turko-Afghan military general Bakhtiyar Khilji's army invaded and burnt down the university. Others believe, that since this ruler was only interested in looting and plundering, he would not have come near a monastery. There is no direct evidence of his having burnt Nalanda. Sadly, the once revered and magnificent university was destroyed and was lost in time.

Scottish surgeon, geographer and surveyor Francis Buchanan-Hamilton surveyed the site in 1812 when locals told him about some Buddhist artefacts that they found there. He did not connect the relics to Nalanda. Later, Major Markham Kittoe, an archaeologist with ASI, correctly identified the mounds and ruins in nearby Kurkihar. Sir Alexander Cunningham soon started an excavation. By using the travelogues of the Chinese monk Xuanzang,

Cunningham could arrive at the exact location of the Nalanda University in 1861–62.

By being a fountain of knowledge, Nalanda gave rise to many great scholars who used their learning to advantage in their own countries. The art of documentation and copying, the importance of studying original texts and translating them into many languages, the importance of patronage to educational institutions and the culture of sharing knowledge are some of the most important lessons that spread to the world.

When you attend an admission test, think about this – Nalanda was one of the toughest learning centres to get into.

University Notes

University of Bologna, Italy, where teaching began in 1088, is the oldest continuously active university. It did not start as a university, but it was here that the name 'universitas', meaning 'community of teachers and scholars' was first used to describe a large seat of higher studies.

Takshashila and Nalanda are often spoken in the same breath. While both were ancient centres of learning, Takshashila (in present-day Pakistan) was much smaller, both in terms of the size of infrastructure and the number of students, and did not have a hostel for teachers and students, and it was not international in scope.

UPANISHADS

The Vedas and Upanishads are the oldest sacred texts that we have in the Indian subcontinent. If you want to jump straight to Page 185 to read about the Vedas first, because they came first, then please go ahead. Else, here is something about the Vedas in a nutshell (we'll need a humongous nutshell even for a brief note, so let's call this just an introduction). The Vedas, four in number, are believed to be divine thoughts revealed only to the really noble rishis when they were in deep meditation. (Think of these as the inexplicable, clear picture you sometimes get in a dream, about something you have been thinking consciously or subconsciously! It is said that these are a combination of gut feeling, knowledge and the sixth sense.) These revelations were passed on orally from one generation to the next. While Maharishi Veda Vyasa is often given credit for compiling the Vedas, this task must have been done by many people in his name. The Vedas brought together people following different philosophies under one umbrella which came to be called Hinduism. (Have you already read about it on page 81?) So, take note, the Vedas came first, Hinduism much later.

Have you noticed how your textbooks are revised periodically? Even in a subject like mathematics where facts do not change over time (2+2 is always equal to 4) either a chapter is made longer or some portion removed. Similarly, after the four Vedas were composed, our rishis felt that a lot more could be added or altered or explained.

The rishis, always trying to understand their texts better, were not shy of reading between the lines, so to speak, and examined the Vedas thoroughly. The Vedic period had introduced a social order, where people were categorized on the basis of the type of work they did. It was meant to be a systematic division of duties for the benefit of everyone in society. Towards the end of the Vedic period, this formation of classes, called varna, led to imbalances. A kshatriya's children had to be kshatriyas. That is, they had to learn warfare. A brahmin's offspring had to learn the Vedas even if they were interested in commerce like a vaishya or in painting murals like a shudra. The rishis felt that the Vedas needed to be interpreted with more thought and broad-mindedness. But rather than tweak or revise the divine words of the Vedas, they decided to add chapters called Brahmanas, Aranyakas and Upanishads – to explain and simplify the original Vedic compositions.

The word Upanishad literally means 'sitting down beside', referring to the practice of students sitting down near a guru or teacher and learning from them. The Upanishads discuss the nature of God, the individual soul and reality. There are 108 Upanishads, some more important than the others. Unlike the Vedas, the Upanishads are not all in verse. There are stories and conversations between student and teacher, including the Bhagavad Gita – yes, the same one that is also part of the Mahabharata! The Upanishads are like seeds that, when sown under the care of wise people, can grow to be strong trees of wisdom.

Some historians believe that after Alexander's arrival in India in 326 BCE, there was enough opportunity for exchange of ideas between India and Greece. Did the Greeks learn from the Upanishads? Scholars have found remarkable similarities between the writings of Plato (429–347 BCE) and the Upanishads.

The Upanishads are Sanskrit texts. For many centuries, they stayed mostly in India. The Persian language, however, had become known to more people in the West. It was *Sirr-e-Akbar*, the Persian translation of the Upanishads by Dara Shikoh in 1657 that reached Europe. French orientalist Abraham Anquetil-Duperron published it as *Oupnek'hat* around 1801–02.

The German philosopher Schopenhauer and American poets Ralph W. Emerson, Walt Whitman and Henry David Thoreau and many others greatly admired the Upanishads. When Swami Vivekananda spoke about India's sacred scriptures in 1893, Americans were even more attracted to the wisdom of the Upanishads. The British founders of the Asiatic Society also commissioned many works on Indic studies in the 19th century.

Truth Alone Triumphs

It was adopted as the national motto of India on 26 January 1950. What? The words Satyameva Jayate, meaning 'truth alone triumphs'. It is part of a mantra from the Mundaka Upanishad.

VEDIC PHILOSOPHY

The Vedas are amongst the oldest known texts in the world. They do not mention the word 'Hindu' even once but are considered sacred texts by Hindus. What are they? A collection of guidelines in the form of mantras or hymns in praise of the elements we all cannot live without – the sun, the rain, the fire, the wind and the water. Who created the Vedas? It is believed that the Vedas are *apaurusheya*, meaning 'of non-human' origin. The timeless wisdom of the Vedas – and that of the Upanishads that followed – is believed to have been received by enlightened rishis. These rishis were simple people who shared it with the next generation in the form of oral recitations. They were genuinely keen to know the answers to questions such as 'Who am I? What is my role in life? Is there a God? If yes, who is God? Can I be happy all the time?' and so on. In fact, it is believed that the Vedas were revealed to many sages when they were in deep meditation.

Texts such as the Vedas that are sources of 'heard' wisdom and are called Shruti. Who wrote down the Vedas? You may have heard about Maharishi Veda Vyasa. He is believed to have compiled – not written or composed – all the hymns that he had heard from the many rishis and put it together into four sections that became the four Vedas. The Rig Veda, dated to around 1500 BCE is the first and therefore the oldest of the four. Samaveda, Yajurveda and Atharvaveda followed in the next thousand years. The time between c. 1500–c. 500 BCE is called the Vedic period. The gurus would ensure that their students, the shishyas, learnt to recite the Vedas so well that they could do it backwards and forwards with equal ease. The Rig Veda itself has 1,028 hymns and 10,600 verses!

There is much inconclusive debate about who brought the Vedas to India. Was it the nomadic communities of goat and cattle herders from Central Asia who settled in India and named themselves Arya? Did they take over the IVC sites, or did they come peacefully? Was it the Harappans themselves who moved away for some reason and reappeared as Arya, the noble ones? Even with the hot debate, everyone agrees that the Aryans were the first to use Sanskrit, the classical language, to compose and orally transmit the Vedas over hundreds of years.

An important lesson in the Vedas is that all creatures are part of the same universal energy. The Vedas led to the formation of a collection of philosophies that came to be called Hinduism. (More about that on page 81.) Now, how did this vast collection of thoughts – on how the universe came to be, who takes care of us, what our role in life is, what happens after we die, and a thousand others – spread throughout the subcontinent and to many places in the world? Jawaharlal Nehru writes in his book *The Discovery of India* that 'Indian thought penetrated to Greece, through Iran, and influenced some thinkers and philosophers there. Much later, Plotinus (Egyptian-born Greek philosopher of the 3rd century CE) came to the east to study Iranian and Indian philosophy...' Greek ruler Agathocles used the Vedic emblems of Krishna and Balarama on his coins.

Between the 5th and 9th centuries, Indian philosophy in the form of Hinduism and Buddhism both flourished side by side. As these religions spread, so did the essence of the Vedas. At different points, people were confused with the many cults, rituals and beliefs in society. Thinkers like Adi Shankara (c. 788–820 CE) had broad-ranging dialogues to clarify and explain the Vedas. Philosophers like Aurobindo Ghose and Swami Vivekananda spoke about the Vedas, spreading its essence to the Western world. Many people from Europe and America were fascinated by Indian philosophies. Max Müller, a German-born British Orientalist (one who studies the Oriental world) and Indologist (yes, one who studies India) and a champion of Sanskrit, studied the copy of Rig Veda written on birch bark, in the Sharada script, that was sourced from Kashmir. This copy is available at the Bhandarkar Oriental Research Institute, Pune. He wrote a lot about the Vedas.

Why should we read the Vedas? What use is it to us? If you have such questions, then the rishis will be happy. Because questioning in a calm and non-aggressive way is also part of the Vedas.

Even if one does not know Sanskrit, or understand the mantras, listening to the chanting can be quite, well, enchanting! Scientific studies show that the rhythmic chants, like music therapy, reduce anxiety levels, increase focus and improve breathing as much for the chanter as the one who hears it. Give it a try!

WEIGHTS

Long before numerals (get to know more about them on page 3) came to be used, the Harappans were using weights to measure commodities. The weights recovered from several IVC sites are mostly in the form of cubes. They may not look spectacular, but they are an indication of a highly evolved mathematical and business sense. Made out of a stone called chert, the basic denominations were of 1, 2, 4, 8, 16, 32 and 64 units. Then, there were some that were 10 times heavier – 120, 320 and 640. Factors of 100 and 1000 have also been found, up to 12,800 units. One unit was equivalent to approximately 0.85 gm. Some weights recovered were so tiny that they suggest they were used in jeweller's shops.

How did they make it? The stones would be chiselled to get rough cubes. These would then be rubbed on a hard, grainy surface – the same principle as in the use of sandpaper – until they weighed exactly the same as the mass of the standard sample weight. More than the size or shape of the stone, the aim was to see that the mass was kept standard. What's even more impressive is that the weights excavated from different regions like

Mohenjo-daro, Harappa and Chanhu-daro, and belonging to different times are all of the same respective weights.

During the golden era of the IVC between 2300 BCE and 1750 BCE, trade was at its zenith. The prosperity of the times was due to the high trade that happened here both within the vast area of the IVC and beyond it. Trade required standard weights. The weights and measures are believed to have been modified after they reached Persia and Central Asia.

WOOTZ STEEL

What is the most magnetic natural mineral on Earth? Magnetite. Which important metal is extracted from this ore? Iron. And which is the most in-demand alloy of iron? You got it – steel. And why was India called the home of the best steel as early the 3rd century BCE? Because it produced a steel that was called 'shiny iron' and came to be called Wootz steel. Woohoo, quiz done!

'Indian steel' was made around the 6th century BCE in South India, in the Mysore, Malabar and Golconda regions and in Sri Lanka. The smiths (that's what metalworkers are called) heated magnetite along with certain leaves in crucibles. The leaves provided the carbon, converting the iron into steel. It is not sure how the name 'wootz' came about in the Western world, but people believe it may have come from the Kannada and Telugu word for the alloy, *ukku* (often pronounced *wukku*), or from the Tamil *urukku irumbu* (melted iron). *Ukku* to wootz, not convincing? Ah, add a clerical error – in 1794, a sample of the Indian crucible steel was sent to the Royal Society, London, along with a letter describing its use in saws, chisels, swords and rock-cutters. The person made an error while transliterating from the Kannada/Telugu to English, where he made it wootz. The name stuck.

The exact process of making this remarkable crucible steel was probably maintained as a trade secret. When Alexander was in India, he received a gift of a hundred talents of *ferrum candidum*, talent being an ancient unit used to measure gold and silver.

From the shores of India, wootz steel left for other countries. For long, trade in certain precious commodities from India was monopolized by southern Arabian merchants. So, when they took Indian steel to Abyssinia, the traders there did not realize it was from India. They thought it was from China. This was also because of the confusion caused by foreign names – the Chera kingdom of South India did have a trade relationship with the Romans. And 'Chera' may have led to the word 'Seres', the Roman word for China. Eventually, the Romans did start referring to it as *Ferrum indicum*. Like other items considered precious, wootz steel was also subject to duty at the port of Alexandria.

During the Crusade wars between 1096 and 1291, the European Crusaders noticed that the swords of the Muslims were stronger and sharper. They called it Damascus steel blades, not knowing that the metal came from India. Highly talented and skilled workers crafted them in India and in the Middle East. European scientists studying the alloy were stumped – no one knew what had gone into the metal. It was only in 1774 that Swedish chemist Torbern Bergman discovered that steel was an alloy of iron and carbon.

Michael Faraday, the British scientist and 'Father of Electricity', tried to replicate the material several times, but failed. In the process, he did so much work that he came to be called the 'Father of Alloy Steel'!

In the 1820s, French scientist Jean Robert Bréant conducted nearly 300 experiments combining different metals like gold, platinum, uranium, tin, zinc, arsenic with iron to produce Damascus steel. While he too failed to produce it, he was able to conclude that it was carburetted steel.

The mystery and the experiments led to the birth of modern metallurgy. Nothing like a seemingly unsolvable challenge to get the best minds working, right?

XOLITA

Oil lamps have been used for thousands of years, and we cannot find out who invented them and in which part of the world. But some smart humans did figure out that if they dipped a wick in oil and lit the end, they would get a steady source of light for at least a few hours. It was also a way of keeping a source of fire alive in the house – striking flintstones can be quite strenuous and dicey. During the Vedic times, this became a practice and that may explain the practice of lighting a diya at home.

The world was making use of the capillary action of a wick long, long before Leonardo da Vinci studied and recorded the action. Seed and nut oils and even whale oils were used in lamps. But what about the wick? Some people used insects. The Chinese used rice paper, which was made with the straw of rice grass. (The edible rice paper is made with rice gruel.) Flax, the fibre from which linen material is made, was used as a wick. Linen rags too were used for the purpose. Once cotton was discovered, people started making wicks with it. Unlike Europe and the Western world that moved from oil lamps to wax candles, India continued to use oil lamps.

The wick is called *thiri* in Tamil, *batti* and *palita* in Hindi, Bengali, Punjabi and many other languages. But what is it called in Assamese? Aha, finally, we have an Indian word for an object starting with the letter X – *xolita*! Like in the rest of the country, during festivals like Diwali, people here light diyas (called *saaki* in Assamese).

Xossa (meaning 'true'), this note about xolita is just so that the alphabet X does not feel left out of this book!

YOGA

Yoga is one of the most important philosophies that India, or Bharatavarsha, has contributed to the world. Yes, what many may think of as just a set of painful contortions of the body is actually a way of life, a way of thinking that can create balance in our lives. It is a way to still all those cascading waves of thoughts in your head.

Let's go back a few thousand years. Roughly, 3,000 years ago, there existed a form of yogic practice in the north-western regions of India, during the Vedic period. Around 1000 BCE, the main themes of yoga started being mentioned in Vedic literature. The first known mention of yoga is in the Rig Veda, the oldest of the four Vedas. A few centuries later, the ideas associated with yoga found a place in the Upanishads. By now, our ancestors had started adding their own rules to the practice, with each person doing it in a different way. It was Maharishi Patanjali who first gathered the philosophy and nature of yoga into a treatise called *Yoga Sutra*. Though he did not invent yoga, he is regarded as the founder of the organized system of modern yoga. There are many legends about him and his birth. Was he born in the 3rd century BCE or in the 4th century CE? His life and times, his place of birth and almost everything about him remains a mystery, but the work attributed to him has lived on till the present. All the branches of yoga have evolved from this one work, generating different schools of thought and practice.

The word 'yoga' comes from the Sanskrit work 'yuj' meaning to bind, join and yoke. It came to mean a practice that could control mind, body, the senses and breath to help attain harmony. Yoga recognizes eight steps to attain perfect balance in life and is therefore called ashtanga yoga (*ashta* = eight, *anga* = limb): yama (universal moral commandments, like you shall not steal from another), *niyama* (purification by self-discipline: so, brush your teeth every day), asana (posture; don't slouch in front of the TV), pranayama (breathe properly; not like a panting dog), pratyahara (training the mind not to be affected by exterior objects; that urge to binge on chips – uh uh), dharana (concentration: yes, please finish your homework first), dhyana (meditation; try not to think of eleven things at the same time), and samadhi (the ultimate practice of meditation).

How did the world come to know about the beauty of yoga? While many spiritual leaders like Adi Shankaracharya (c. 788 CE–820 CE), Ramakrishna Paramahamsa (1836–86), Ramana Maharshi (1879–1950), Paramahansa Yogananda (1893–1952), practised and promoted yoga, it was Swami Vivekananda's speech at the World's Parliament of Religions in Chicago in 1893 that put yoga firmly on the world map. He spoke about the unity of all religions. His speech made such an impact that people came to India to learn yoga from the best of gurus. They went back to their countries and started practising and teaching yoga. One of them came all the way from Latvia (then a part of Russia) to become the first woman to study under Guru Krishnamacharya in the Mysore Maharaja's palace, where B.K.S. Iyengar was her batchmate, changed her name from Eugenie Peterson to Indra Devi and went on to teach yoga in China, and later in Hollywood, USA.

In 2015, the United Nations declared 21 June, the day of the summer solstice – the longest day in the year in the northern hemisphere – as International Yoga Day. Earth gets the greatest energy from the sun on this day. And humans get a lot of energy if they practise yoga consistently, calmly and in the prescribed way.

Zero

If someone asked you what you knew about Brahmagupta, and you shrugged your shoulders and answered 'nothing', you would be... right! He is known for a lot of things, like finding the almost accurate distance between the Earth and the Moon, that the Earth moved around the Sun and not the other way around and the method to solve an equation. The most useful thing Brahmagupta of Bhillamala (now Bhinmal, Rajasthan) gave to the world was the concept of zero. No, he did not invent it, but he did show very neatly that *shunya* is an important number. You could say, he made something really big out of nothing.

Shunya in Sanskrit means 'void', or 'nothing', and comes from the root word meaning 'hollow'. The idea of putting a dot as a placeholder may have been experimented by the Sumers in 300 BCE, but they did not take it further. Ancient Indians who had invented the 'nine signs', or the earliest numerals in Brahmi script had also started using *shunya* as a placeholder. (In the number 2026, the zero as place holder would mean the number has no hundreds.) Acharya Pingala used the concept of *shunya* as a placeholder in his work *Chandashastra* (more about him on page 75). In 1882, archaeologists found 70 pieces of Himalayan birch bark with text containing hundreds of zeroes in a field in Bakhshali, in present-day Pakistan. Radiocarbon dating in 2017 by the scientists at the University of Oxford Bodleian Libraries indicated that the manuscript was from the 3rd or 4th century, while earlier studies had dated it somewhere between 650 to 900 CE. Many scholars say the leaves may have been from an earlier period, but the writing is from around 700 CE. It still makes the Bakhshali zero the oldest recorded on text.

In the year 628 CE, 30-year-old Brahmagupta published the treatise on astronomy called *Brahmasphutasiddhanta* (*The Opening of the Universe*), or simply, *Siddhanta*. He had taken an existing treatise on astronomy and set about correcting and refining it. He had also added many of his own thoughts about mathematical operations in it. He believed that *shunya* was not just a placeholder, but a number on its own. *Shunya* was not 'nothing'. It was, he said in the definition, that which is left when a number is subtracted from itself. It was also the first book in the history of mathematics that spelt out the rules of using what Indians called *shunya*. Now, let's see how it came to be called zero.

After Brahmagupta's death, and over a 100 years later, in 773 CE, Baghdad was a city that was considered a great centre for learning and culture. Scholars gathered here from all over the world to exchange manuscripts, discuss new theories, mostly in astronomy and mathematics. Here, an Indian group of experts presented a valuable gift from the Raja of Sindh to Caliph al-Mansur Abbasid – the essence of Brahmagupta's *Siddhanta*. Whether they took a copy of the book in written form, or as something they knew by memory and could recite freely, is not known. But they were able to explain the contents to the excited foreigners. The caliph saw the importance of this treatise and immediately commissioned his chief astronomer Muhammad al-Fazari to create an Arabic translation. This was how the Arab world came to know about *shunya*. The Arabic translation made it *sifr*. The Venetians made it *zefiro*, and the French made it zero. It entered the English language in the 1600s as zero too.

The Arabs were great traders and soon adopted the *sifr* in their accounting. Not so the Europeans. When Fibonacci, the mathematician who had learnt all about Arabic numerals and their magic from a Moorish teacher, and others brought the idea to Italy, the people wanted nothing to do with it. Even 400 years after Indians and Arabs started using zero, European governments were wary. What if cheats added an extra zero or two? The Italian city of Florence banned the use of zero.

Even when Europe did start using zero, they assumed that all ten digits were Arabic and called them Arabic numbers. It was George Cœdès, the French scholar of Southeast Asian archaeology and history, who discovered the Eastern origin of zero. He was translating a bill of transaction inscribed on a stele (you could call it a stone slab) in Cambodia. The date on the bill was inscribed as 605, corresponding to 683 CE in the modern calendar. This was before the Arabs had spread their mathematical work. His work aimed to prove that zero was not of Arabic origin. The Indian zero has travelled not just west, but also east, and is a mathematical hero all over the world.

Oldest Zero Inscription in India

Many of the texts and manuscripts of ancient India are lost forever. What we do have are copies of copies. That is why anything written on stone still makes the best evidence of proof. The oldest known '0' inscribed on stone in India is at the Chaturbhuj Temple, dated 876 CE, in the Gwalior Fort, Madhya Pradesh. The oldest inscription of zero on a stone slab is housed at the ancient temple of Angkor Wat. It once adorned the walls of a 7th-century temple on Mekong River, Cambodia.

ACKNOWLEDGEMENTS

Namaste! Thank you for reading this.

On a hot afternoon in 2024, in a barren stretch of land, I stood looking at things retrieved from an Iron Age, megalithic archaeological site in Adichanallur, Tamil Nadu. River Thamirabarani flowed close by carrying with it the tales of ancient merchants and precious wares. This was my first visit to an archaeological prehistoric site. I had just finished the manuscript of *Travelling Treasures: 100 Incredible Tales of How Things Came to India.*

Already in awe of inventors, discoverers and other brilliant people, I came away from this site fascinated by human ingenuity and history. The site was first discovered by a German Dr Fedor Jagor. Englishman Alexander Rea excavated it in 1889 and Frenchman Louis Lapicque did another excavation in 1904. And here I was, an Indian, looking into India's Iron Age.

My first note of thanks is therefore to all the people, all over the world, irrespective of their nationality, who work tirelessly, literally digging for information that makes the past clearer for us. While doing the research for *Travelling Treasures*, I found many things that had their beginnings in India. I started listing them, just out of interest.

And then, my editor Sanya Verma asked me a few months later if I would like to write *Travelling Treasures* 2.0. Again, I wondered if I could find enough credible information to write a book! While *Travelling Treasures* was mostly about tangible 'things' that came to India, what went out to the world from India and undivided India were more abstract, more intangible – philosophies, knowledge systems, life lessons. To write *Travelling Treasures* 2.0, one had to first try to understand these philosophies better. It involved reading and more reading and pondering over the ideas.

This would not have been possible without the most important books available – very often, free of charge – online, thanks to digital initiatives across the world. A big thank you to all the people involved in democratizing knowledge.

To these people, not in alphabetical order, thank you!

- Sanya Verma, my editor at Hachette India, for trusting me with a sequel to *Travelling Treasures*. I could not have written this book without your quiet resolve, calm worldview and down-to-earth comments.
- Samiksha Gosain, Naman Arya, Sini Nair and the team at Hachette India for your constant cheering. Shaurya Sircar for the editing and fact-checking.
- Vibha Surya for serving us the world on a cover, and the little illustrations in the book.
- Dr Pradeep Chakravarthy, author and historian, for insisting I visit Adichanallur.
- Readers and reviewers of *Travelling Treasures* who wrote good things about the book and hoped that a second one was on the anvil.
- Bookstore people, teachers, librarians, literature festival organizers, for putting me in front of children –

their questions and views are what drives a writer to do better.

- The family – members from different countries whose stories over the years have fed my imagination and facilitated my virtual travels.
- Friends and family who good-naturedly declared my social media feed was getting too predictable – yay, folks, now I have a new book to crow about!

Finally, to the important message in the Bhagavad Gita, Chapter 18, Verse 63:

'*Vimrsyaitad asesena yatheccchasi tatha kuru.*'

'Fully THINK (ponder) on what I said and then do as YOU deem fit.'

While the writing of this book has made me even more proud of being an Indian, I hope I will have the humility and the generosity to never forget that there is greatness in each country and in every religion. We may have given a lot to the world, but we have also received a lot.

Dear reader, thank you for picking up this book. Happy travels!

SELECTED BIBLIOGRAPHY

Acharya, K.T. A *Historical Dictionary of Indian Food.* Delhi: Oxford University Press, 1998.

Bhishagratna, K.L. *An English Translation of The Sushrutha Samhita.* Calcutta: Wilkins Press, 1907.

Agarwal, Deepa. *The Arthashastra for Children.* Gurugram: Puffin Books, 2023.

Bechmann, Johann. *A History of Inventions and Discoveries.* London: Printed for Longman, Hurst, Rees, Orme, and Brown, 1817.

Da Orta, Garcia. *Colloquies on the Simples & Drugs of India.* London: Henry Sotheran & Co., 1913.

Darympl, William. *The Golden Road: How Ancient India Transformed the World.* London: Bloomsbury, 2024.

Mookerji, R.K. *Chandragupta Maurya and His Times.* Madras: G. S. Press, 1943.

Murray, Hugh. *The Travels of Marco Polo.* Edinburgh: Oliver & Boyd, 1844.

Pai, Roopa. *The Yoga Sutras for Children.* Gurugram: Hachette India, 2023.

Pai, Roopa. *Vedas and Upanishads for Children.* Gurugram: Hachette India, 2023.

Schoff, Wilfred Harvey, English Translation. *The Periplus of the Erythraean Sea: travel and trade in the Indian Ocean.* New York: Longman's Green and Co., 1912.

SELECT LIST OF WEB LINKS

All websites last accessed on 1 January 2026.

'History shows that Bharatavarsha has not always been the same thing as the country of India', Scroll.in. https://scroll.in/article/852113/history-shows-that-bharatavarsha-has-not-always-been-the-same-thing-as-the-country-of-india

'Amla: An Ancient Super Berry Emerges From India', Clinical Education. https://www.clinicaleducation.org/resources/reviews/amla-an-ancient-super-berry-emerges-from-india/

'Did You Know? The Influence of Astrology on the Science of Astronomy on the Science of Astronomy along the Silk Roads', unesco.org.

'The UNESCO Silk Roads Programme', Unesco.org. https://en.unesco.org/silkroad/content/did-you-know-influence-astrology-science-astronomy-along-silk-roads

'Evolution of medical education in India: The impact of colonialism'. National Library of Medicine. https://pmc.ncbi.nlm.nih.gov/articles/PMC5105212/

The roots of legacy: A visit to 'Thanjavur Quartet's house', https://www.thehindu.com/features/friday-review/dance/The-roots-of-legacy-A-visit-to-Thanjavur-Quartets-house/article14588983.ece

'Understanding kumkumam', Paticheri.com. https://www.paticheri.com/2020/10/17/understanding-kumkumam/

'Pakadarpanam: Nala Maharaja's Culinary Masterpiece from Ancient India', The Culture Heritage of India blog. https://cultureandheritage.

org/2023/05/pakadarpanam-nala-maharajas-culinary-masterpiece-from-ancient-india.html

'What is a bodhisattva? A scholar of Buddhism explains', The Conversation. https://theconversation.com/what-is-a-bodhisattva-a-scholar-of-buddhism-explains-189366

'Mehsi Button Industry', East Champaran website. https://eastchamparan.nic.in/mehsi-button-industry/

'Gold Button', Harappa.com. https://www.harappa.com/indus3/301.html

'Rooted in Racism: Cardamom', https://www.heifer.org/blog/rooted-in-racism-cardamom.html

'Evolution of Payment Systems in India', Archive.org. https://web.archive.org/web/20190120043055/https://m.rbi.org.in/Scripts/PublicationsView.aspx?id=155

'An Introduction: Botany, Origin and Diversity', CABI Digital Library. https://www.cabidigitallibrary.org/doi/10.1079/9781789249736.0001

'Cotton, A Global History: Spinning tales', Weatherhead Centre, Harvard University. https://www.wcfia.harvard.edu/publications/cotton-global-historyspinning-tales

'The Word *Curry* Came From a Colonial Misunderstanding', *The Atlantic*. https://www.theatlantic.com/health/archive/2019/04/why-we-call-indian-dishes-curry-colonial-history/586828/

'The Art of Cookery', Archive.org. https://archive.org/details/TheArtOfCookery/page/n105/mode/2up?q=currey

'Susruta Samhita: A Scientific Synopsis', Archive.org. https://archive.org/details/susruta-samhita-a-scientific-synopsis-priyadaranjan-ray-hirendranath-gupta-mira-roy/page/3/mode/2up?q=Atharvaveda

'What is the Fibonacci sequence?', *Live Science*. https://www.livescience.com/37470-fibonacci-sequence.html

'The importance (and baggage) of ghee', *Down to Earth*. https://www.downtoearth.org.in/food/the-importance-and-baggage-of-ghee-87379

'Champaran Satyagraha: A revolution of consciousness,' mkgandhi.org. https://www.mkgandhi.org/articles/champaran-satyagraha.php

'Ibn Battuta, the Jackfruit and Mexico', Points of Departure blog. https://pointsofdeparture.wordpress.com/2012/05/29/ibn-battuta-the-jackfruit-and-mexico/

'Historical Background of the Jataka', wisdomlib.org. https://www.wisdomlib.org/buddhism/essay/animals-in-buddhism/d/doc1460949.html

'The fascinating and enduring world of Rudyard Kipling's *The Jungle Book*', scroll.in. https://scroll.in/reel/802069/the-fascinating-and-enduring-world-of-rudyard-kiplings-the-jungle-book

'The Jute Story', Heritagepedia blog. https://recoveringsouthasianhistory.wordpress.com/2022/05/15/the-jute-story-from-empire-to-oblivion-and-back/

'Your khaki pants have a history that may surprise you', *National Geographic*. https://www.nationalgeographic.com/history/article/surprising-colonial-history-khakis

'Navigating the Menaka-Archive', menaka-archive.org. https://www.projekt-mida.de/reflexicon/navigating-the-menaka-archive/

Rediscover the Ancient Game of Chaupar', historified.in. https://historified.in/2024/05/25/rediscover-the-ancient-game-of-chaupar-a-timeless-journey-of-strategy-and-culture/

'Thank Plate Tectonics for Tasty Oranges', *Discover*. https://www.discovermagazine.com/thank-plate-tectonics-for-tasty-oranges-37444

'Madras Checks', Art and Photography Foundation. https://imp-art.org/articles/madras-checks/

'When cloth maketh a city', *The Hindu*. https://www.thehindu.com/news/cities/chennai/when-cloth-maketh-a-city/article3792732.ece

'Romancing the Mango', *Goya Journal*. https://www.goya.in/blog/romancing-the-mango-the-story-on-indias-most-beloved-fruit

'How Namaste Flew Away From Us', npr.org. https://www.npr.org/sections/codeswitch/2020/01/17/406246770/how-namaste-flew-away-from-us

'A Beloved Bitterness', *Whetstone Magazine*. https://www.whetstonemagazine.com/south-asia-journal/a-beloved-bitterness

'The Orange's Origin', scmp.com. https://www.scmp.com/magazines/post-magazine/short-reads/article/3209219/oranges-origins-how-it-travelled-east-west-and-its-name-evolved

'History of Migration of Panchatantra and what it can teach us', Institute of Oriental Study Thane. https://www.orientalthane.com/speeches/speech2008.htm

'Pepper, the Black Gold', *UpperCrust*. https://uppercrustindia.com/v3/posts/1129/pepper-the-black-gold

'The Manipur Origins of Modern Polo', *Deccan Herald*. https://www.deccanherald.com/features/art-and-culture/the-manipur-origins-of-modern-polo-3360125

'The Indian Sulbasutras', Math History blog. https://mathshistory.st-andrews.ac.uk/HistTopics/Indian_sulbasutras/

'The Development of Rain Gages', thirdworldcentre.org. https://thirdworldcentre.org/1967/09/development-of-rain-gages/

'Chanakya's existence, Ashoka's politics', theprint.in. https://theprint.in/pageturner/book-scene/chanakyas-existence-ashokas-politics-new-book-has-stories-and-counter-stories-on-mauryas/1272722/

'The Evolution of the Indian Sari', Indiacurrents.com. https://indiacurrents.com/the-evolution-of-the-indian-sari/

'Seeking Seamless Celestial Globes'. Foundation for Science Technology and Civilisation. https://www.muslimheritage.com/uploads/Seeking%20Seamless%20Celestial%20Globes.pdf

'How Moksha Patam Rolled Into Snakes and Ladders', Azim Premji University podcast. https://azimpremjiuniversity.edu.in/thats-the-thing/how-moksha-patam-rolled-into-snakes-and-ladders

'Sugar and the Rise of the Plantation System', World History Encyclopedia. https://www.worldhistory.org/article/1784/sugar--the-rise-of-the-plantation-system/

'Turmeric, The Golden Spice: From Asia to Africa', irispublishers.com. https://irispublishers.com/oajaa/fulltext/turmeric-the-golden-spice-from-asia-to-africa.ID.000540.php

'A New Book Shows How Nalanda Mahavihara Contributed to the Fields of Ancient Mathematics and Astronomy', scroll.in. https://scroll.in/article/1077528/a-new-book-shows-how-nalanda-mahavihara-contributed-to-the-fields-of-ancient-mathematics-astronomy

'Early Weights and Weighing in Egypt and the Indus Valley', jstor.org. https://www.jstor.org/stable/4171634?read-now=1#page_scan_tab_contents

'Linguistic Avatars of Wootz', infinityfoundation.com. https://www.infinityfoundation.com/mandala/t_es/t_es_agraw_wootz_frameset.htm